Phebe Davis

# The travels and experience of Miss Phebe B. Davis of Barnard

Being a sequel to her two years and three months in the N.Y. State

Phebe Davis

**The travels and experience of Miss Phebe B. Davis of Barnard**
*Being a sequel to her two years and three months in the N.Y. State*

ISBN/EAN: 9783337210618

Printed in Europe, USA, Canada, Australia, Japan

Cover: Foto ©Andreas Hilbeck / pixelio.de

More available books at **www.hansebooks.com**

# THE TRAVELS AND EXPERIENCE

OF

# MISS PHEBE B. DAVIS,

OF

BARNARD, WINDSOR COUNTY, VT.,

BEING A SEQUEL TO HER

## Two Years and Three Months

IN THE

## N. Y. STATE LUNATIC ASYLUM,

AT UTICA, N. Y.

"BE JUST AND FEAR NOT."

PRICE, TWENTY-FIVE CENTS.

SYRACUSE, N. Y.:
J. G. K. TRUAIR & CO., STEREOTYPERS AND PRINTERS.
1860.

SYRACUSE, *July* 1, 1860.

THE bearer of this note—Miss Phebe Davis—has been an acquaintance of ours for the last fourteen years.

Her character for a conscientious determination to do right, in all circumstances, may be depended upon.

Her health is her apology for offering this book to the public; she hopes that the avails will give her the means of support.

She seems, also, to have a strong desire to benefit the condition of those who have been afflicted with her.

|  |  |
|---|---|
| GROVE LAWRENCE, | MRS. GROVE LAWRENCE, |
| O. R. STRONG, | A. B. SHIPMAN, M. D. |
| JOS. F. SABINE, | M. D. BURNET, |
| E. BALDWIN, | B. D. NOXON. |

# PREFACE.

Perhaps I cannot say anything that will interest community; but this work is rather a continuation of the one that I have written on the Lunatic Asylum, at Utica, N. Y.,—together with a short chapter on mechanism, and the outlines of my travels in twenty-five States in the Union, including most of the Southern States; and the reader will find every feature of Slavery shown up just as I found it, and also a true account of my false imprisonment in Charleston, S. C.

P. B. D.

# SEQUEL TO TWO YEARS
### IN THE
# N. Y. STATE LUNATIC ASYLUM.

### CHAPTER I.

I am a native of the State of Vermont, Windsor County, and town of Barnard; brought up in a farmer's kitchen; well acquainted with the wash-tub and the cheese-press, and not a stranger to the milking of a few cows, if necessary; and in that section of the country it was fashionable to eat; and the soil and climate was not prolific of a class of people that was ashamed to cook what was necessary to supply the demands of the physical system—and I am rather a unique in the world, but always everywhere present—and I partook of the vulgar habit of cooking, with the rest of the Yankees. And the parlor work was not piano playing, but knitting and sewing; and in the sitting-room, perhaps, one would find a spinning-wheel or two, which often made the domestic circle appear very social. But how little I knew at the time that they were my only happy days—when I could run down cellar and get any quantity of the best kind of apples, and a plenty of cider, and then up stairs after butternuts; and what could be more desirable to a numerous family of young children than that class of associates? To be sure, I would not wish to go back there to live, but "there is no place like home."

Who can obliterate local associations? There is the same old brook running past the house now, that has for more than fifty years past, and the same old well that invites old friends to "partake of the waters of life freely." Yet it's not pleasant to dwell on the past, or at least on the dark side of the past. But, my mother died when I was about the age of seven years, and I was soon under the influence of one that did not understand my composition; and as the tide of life ebbs and flows, I happened to be thrown upon my own resources, with a positive mind and living for a fixed motive that I gathered up when I was about seventeen years of age—which was, to write a book, and some unseen agency told me that I should get my living by a feeble production of my own; but the whole world have doubled their diligence to turn the current of thought and action, but all without success on their part, as I felt impelled to pursue the course that looked consistent to myself. I have had to "stoop to conquer," but where there is no army there is no victory. I know my own weak points, but I have studied to know my strong points, and I am a victim of sectarian circumstances, which is my only apology for the past. God would not give me power to send my head back to him, and get it made over to fit the social condition of society nor the pious straight-jackets of the nineteenth century, which is made up of devotion, but no religion. The fact is, each sect coins their own trap to catch game in, and those that dupe the most are the best fellows. The ministers address their arguments to the base of the brain, and "like begets like," and church-going christians are magnetized into a certain class of belief that just fits their phrenological developments, which is nothing more nor less than a species of foreign barbarism; but the most of them are like the Indians in one respect—their superstition predominates over their reason. They have always been willing to live in a h—ll in this beautiful world for the sake of securing themselves a better place in the world to come; but if they should fail on getting a through ticket to the land of rest, it would be like children trying to overtake their own shadow by moonlight;

and I think it foolish to avoid a certainty for an uncertainty. I want a Heaven on earth, and the whole is summed up in the golden rule, which is, to do by another as you would that another would do unto you, which is the only true religion in the world, and the only religion that Jesus Christ established on earth. And how much less it would cost the world to carry out the principle of universal benevolence, than it now does to furnish Churches and the variety of Public Institutions that I consider one of the great burdens of society.

But nobody must speak to be heard, except a few that are called great men in the world, and the most of that class are great in some respects, but in others they are very weak, and their weak points are always connected with their selfishness, which leaves them blind to their own motives. And the most of that class of men think if a Lady ventures out of her kitchen to speak, that she is quite out of her own sphere of action. I know that the women in Syracuse have not treated me very well, but there are good women in the land, and there would be many more such if they could be allowed their just rights; but as they now are, they are better than no women, for I should be very loth to live in a world where there were no women. It would be a chilly atmosphere to me to annihilate women; there would be a state of semi-barbarism in less than two hours. Women are to the world what the pilot is to the steamboat; yet there are household tyrants in both classes, and petty tyrants in every avenue in life; but the most of women are nothing but voluntary slaves to their husbands, instead of companions, as they should be. When I survey their social condition, I do not wonder that they live for sinister motives; but if they were properly educated, they would be capable of acting the best parts in the great amphitheatre of human affairs. But the ministers are the first to oppose equal rights, for they know very well that they get their support through the influence of the women; but who ever knew a good man that did not have a good mother? Napoleon Bonaparte said that we needed intelligent mothers, but when shall we see that class of mothers? Not at present, for they are only partially educated; but I hope in mercy that the next crop of mothers will not furnish the world with as many criminals as the present generation has, but after all, I consider criminals victims of circumstances. The Clergy costs the United States six millions annually, and the criminals nineteen millions, and I believe the greatest of the two classes occupy the pulpit. There are a great many crimes committed every day, which, if recognized by law, would swell the number of convicts in all the criminal Institutions in the United States; and there are thousands in prison to-day for less crime than half of the world are guilty of, that are now at large; but the first cause of crime is only winked at as yet. When the human family cease to rob each other of their natural rights, then will crime cease to exist. I have been a great sufferer by the wrongs of the world, which has led me to investigate the cause of all classes of crimes as far as I have had an opportunity of studying character, and I have arrived at the conclusion that "those that are without sin had better cast the first stone," for no one person is made of perfection, and the lowest class of people in the world have redeeming traits of character; but they have become low by associations; and if there were less legal robbers, there would be less vulgar ones. And how many dollars have I received at the hands of great, noble souls, encased in the poor man, and even classes that did not claim a standing in society have contributed their share very liberally; and I hope that I have gratitude enough to appreciate a small favor from a great soul. I found many individuals that could not buy a book of me, but perhaps hand me a dime or half-dime, and I took the will for the deed; and I very seldom met with ill or abrupt treatment from such as are called the lower classes; but was much more apt to find vulgar minds in high life, and I know that no principle will ever redeem the vices of the fallen except general intelligence and genuine philanthropy.

Some author has said that the world will talk about religion, and write about it, and fight about it, and die for it, and do everything except live religion. The religion of Jesus Christ has got rather old-fashioned, and any shrewd man can coin a piety to suit any class of people that will pay him the most money for his preaching ; and I often meet them, and many of them are very impudent to me, and I have told some of them that my own religion was more useful to me than theirs, for mine was worth making sacrifices for, but theirs was not.

It is now twenty-one years since people found out that I was crazy, and all because I could not fall in with every vulgar belief that was fashionable. I never could be led by everything and everybody, simply because they all told me their arguments were right, and at the same time they were all in direct opposition to each other, and I knew that all truths harmonized. I kept track of all the Churches in Syracuse for a number of years, and I found that they all persecuted each other. They all coin their own Deity and their own demons; and each one according to the brain that they have to do it with, " and the man that does best is best." Each man's brain should be his only Church, and then he can worship in spirit and in truth, and he will find it will cost him much less to worship God than it now does. The religion of Jesus Christ should be established in each one's own head, for a well-balanced brain is a great Institution. But Sectarianism in its different phases has chilled my blood into icicles, and my heart has become ossified, but there is just one corner of it that is able to perform its office. And I should be very glad to meet with a change of heart now, if I could get a sound one, for there is danger of my dying with the heart disease, and then the ministers would say, " Poor soul ! she has gone into eternity unprepared !" and they could slander my soul at their leisure, and I could not talk back.

It appears that Jesus Christ healed the sick and restored the blind to sight, and cured the insane, but he did not do it by the use of medicines—such as pills and blisters, and bleeding—but the healing sanitive was in his own kind philanthropic nature ; he had the principle of love, which is the strongest principle that exists in nature ; he did not come to save the righteous, but call sinners to repentance, and his nature was so pure that he did not feel contaminated by associating with the degraded, because his motive was to do them good by his example, and he did make them better, but he made himself unpopular by doing good in the world; and I wish that we had a few physicians now that could heal by the same principle that Christ did; and I am thinking that Doctors' bills would be small compared with what they now are. I think that the most of cases of insanity are curable, if the cause could be removed; but the treatment in Asylums is generally addressed to the effect, and the cause still exists— the true cause is not always known. My own nervous system was thrown out of balance by external surroundings, but medicine did not reach my case—neither did a long confinement in the Lunatic Asylum do it, for there were no healing qualities in Dr. Benedict nor Dr. Gray,— and Dr. Cook was very young, but rather gentlemanly; and Dr. Porter knew more than the other three, but he left soon after I went there.

Mr. Rhodes, the first steward, and Dr. Porter were cousins, and they were very much respected in the Institution. And Dr. Headly was there a short time, but he had so much sympathy in his nature that he could not live there, for no person can live there unless they like to witness misery; and the class that apply for situations in public institutions are generally the lower classes, that are not qualified for usefulness anywhere, and the most of Drs. that are employed in lunatic asylums do much more to aggravate the disease than they do to cure it. And after I had been through all the pious mills, and crazy mills, and rational mills, I found myself a living skeleton, without means of support or a home, and my strength was all invested in my will power, and I made that my only starting-point when I left the Institution; but I kept rather still, for fear I should get outwitted, and in selling my books I found a few individuals that had humanity enough to be capable of restoring the equilibrium of the nervous system to its proper balance; and just as long as I was under kind influences I was perfectly passive, and kindness has been my only medicine. And if the great brotherhood of mankind would all extend the hand of kindness and charity to each other, there would soon be less misery in the world. In traveling, I have visited a great many public institutions of both kinds, both benevolent and criminal, and I rather think that the most of them are perfect pandemoniums; but I wish I could think better of them than I do, but I judge from what I know, and in the Lunatic Asylum I know that a positive mind would live surrounded by the same class of influences that a negative mind could not live in any length of time, for the positive mind will repel disease, while the negative will partake of it. Although my own nerves have been very well kinked up, I have in a measure straightened them out again; but how bad some have felt to see me getting my living again, and they have pulled on every string to hedge up my path; but at length, I believe, they have fallen back into the negative state, and agreed to allow me the privilege of getting an honest living—for, in times past, they would neither help me nor allow me to help myself, and they appeared determined to prevent my writing my other book; but Mrs. Philo Ray allowed me the privilege of writing it in her family, and I am now with her daughter, Mary, while writing again; but when I wrote the other pamphlet I put forth a very great mental effort, for it was necessity in the extreme that called that small work out of my brains, and the mental suffering that I endured while writing that book is utterly indescribable, from different causes. The prominent cause was in my head. My brain appeared to be too large for my skull, and there was no reaching the cure except by external influences; but Mrs. Ray and all her family were very kind to me, but I knew, if I did not sell the book, that the poor-house was the only home I could claim; but my feelings told me that the book would sell just as it did, and I thought I had paid for a living, and I thought I merited a living. My hope is small, but my faith is very large, and in less than one week after I had finished that book, my head felt like another head, and I often looked in the glass to see if it was my own that I was wearing about, but I could not deny the face, and began to feel much more reconciled to the condition that my head was in. The nervous system will resist a great many shocks, "but a continual dropping will wear stone." One of the most terrible deaths that the Spanish Inquisition ever inflicted on a person, was by causing one drop of water at a time to fall on the top of the head until it would produce a very great state of suffering.

But a poor person that lives for exalted motives, must expect to live in a world of their own, and my world for a time was in a cell in the Lunatic Asylum, and I arranged the most of my other pamphlet while in that cold, chilly cell; the stench was terrible; and during the time I was locked up in that cell, the Doctor sent me an emetic, and the first food after that was cold corned beef and cold boiled potato, and baker's bread and cold water. I partook of the sacrament, but left the beef and potato until I got well enough to partake of all that I could get there. Some of the help in the Asylum told me that Dr. Benedict would get up in the morning long before his wife did, and pray for himself and children, and let her do her own praying;—I told the girls I did not wonder that she chose to do her own praying, if she knew him as well as we did; and they said he always blessed his food before eating, and he could well afford to tell God how good it was, for he had the best the market afforded, and we only had second and third class eatables, and got it at our own expense, too. I wonder how much money it has cost the City of Syracuse to try to govern me; and they have never put me under the supervision of one yet that could govern themselves; I can do that, and always could when I chose; but there are circumstances where "forbearance ceases to be a virtue;" for human endurance is not made of India-rubber, although my own is rather elastic, for I always meant to convert my misfortunes into success— that is all the ability that I happen to possess, which will allow me to provide for myself, for real high souled people are but little appreciated in this world—they are never respected until they have been dead two or three hundred years. It has been said that one of our prominent authors wrote the best work that he ever wrote in his life to defray the expenses of his mother's funeral! And who can wonder that the depth of that full-grown soul was called out on such an occasion as that, and I presume that he coined that soul into truths and gave them form, and by the use of language presented them to the world in that peculiar manner that was not to be resisted!

As for my own small productions, I have never thought them great; neither have I ever thought them very interesting; but I claim they are true, and there is the only merit in my disconnected class of ideas that I offer to the public. But I write by impression, and it's worth everything to me to know that my impressions have never deceived me, while all my friends thought I was pursuing the wrong course. It was riveted in my mind that it would result in my favor at the end of a certain time; and sure enough, I have realized all my anticipations so far—thank Heaven for that. During the time that I was in that dismal cell in the Asylum, suffering with cold and hunger, and not even a chair to sit in, and no bed in the cell, and not able to sit up, I made the best use of the naked floor that I could, and my bed and pillow was the floor for a number of weeks. One side of the cell was ceiled up with narrow boards, which were varnished; and in that very cell I discovered traces of some great genius. It was the work of some female, done with a hair-pin, which was the drawing of a splendid carriage and four horses, all harnessed, and the driver on his seat with the lines in his hands, and even the whip was on his side. And I thought that I never saw a picture that looked more life-like than that did; and the artist was confined in one of the worst halls in the Asylum. But society is arbitrary, and no great genius can act unnatural; and a great portion of those that are qualified by nature to do these acts end either in some Prison or a Lunatic Asylum, and their influence is lost to the world, while the aristocratic sins, and even in Congress they remind me of a family of small children at meal time, quarrelling to see which shall have the largest piece of pie; and for the same cause, I do believe, they are guilty of in Washington every year. They would arrest the lower classes, as they are called, and pitch them into the watch-house, and the next morning the daily paper tells the criminal news; but the working class are paying men at a dear rate for fighting one half of their time and quarreling the other half. It's only a few years since I read of their spending six weeks' time talking about a Door-keeper, and as crazy as I am, I could select a man to fill that office in fifteen minutes; and if their salary was very small, they would despatch business faster than they do now, but their motives are on a level with highway robbery "But," as Henry Ward Beecher says, "they can all pray cream, and live skimmed milk," and I do not wonder that they are all afraid to meet the King of Terrors, as they talk of, but I always thought there was more terror in this world than in the other; for the "love of God casteth off fear." And I can truly say that I have never known what fear was yet. "It's fear that makes our demons, and weak hope our God." And I choose to make my own impressions in preference to being led; yet I like to learn of all, but not to be governed by any, and I like to consult the wise and then do as I choose; but I do not ask any person to adopt my opinions, but simply ask all to believe that I am honest in them myself— that is what I call honorable generosity. I do not call others dishonest because they cannot think just as I do, but we all have claims on each other's civility; there is no argument in favor of our abusing each other because we do not all look just alike; and, as the Indian said, if we all thought alike, we would all want his squaw. But how many great men have written out their lives in prison, because they were made legally responsible for thought; and when I was in the asylum they locked me up when they pleased, but what did I care for that as long as they had no key that would fit my mouth. I knew that I should live through it all, and I told them I should, and that when I got out they would hear from me.

## CHAPTER II.

"The battle is not always for the strong, nor the race for the swift." It seems a great pity that the human family have never had the privilege of establishing the law of self-government in each and every one's nature; for Sabbath-day government costs a man a great deal of money, and it's the working class that supports the fashionable net-work of hypocrisy, and when a rich man gives the minister a liberal donation, he prays for the rich man and tells God how good the man was to him, and perhaps the same week he has cheated some poor man out of nearly every cent that he was worth to get what he gave the minister, and the poor man is forgotten in prayer-time. Our first thanks for what we get to eat, drink, and wear, belong to Deity, and the next to the working class; but there is a great many wealthy people that work hard, and I like to see them enjoy themselves; but I like to see a person become master of his own thoughts, for one man's head is the greatest Institution that ever emanated from Deity, and yet the most of the world will allow their skull to be made a rag-bag of to throw all the loose rubbish into, and one cannot establish a philosophical fact in a cranium that is already full of old rags; but just empty out the refuse, and then there is room for good sense;—there is so much intricacy in the class that wants to rule, that it takes a person of very observing mind, and one well posted in human nature, to comprehend their motives; and if an individual does dive deep enough to understand them, and has moral courage sufficient to tell them what they are, the next news is, there is an order made out to take them to the Lunatic Asylum.

There are many people that retain very much that they hear, but they never digest anything, for they have not the ability to compare and arrange a class of ideas that are fit for every day practical use; but a all blunder along, hit or miss. But "order is heaven's first law." Christ established the great principle of love and morality, and as soon as the mass of mankind get wise enough to establish order, then we can have a harmonious world, for love and morality and order will produce harmony, and we can all have a Heaven on earth—then comes the Millennium. I am often asked the question what my belief is in regard to the future state, and I will now answer the question. In the first place, man is older than any book that there is in the world, and the Bible requires us to prepare to live, not to prepare to die, for the class of men that wrote the Bible knew very well that when a person was fit to stay in this world, they were fit to go into the other; and I believe we shall enjoy just as much Heaven in the future world as we carry out of the present world, and I presume we shall find it a state of the mind instead of the unpleasant locality that it has been represented to be. I always leave out the sulphur, for I do not think Heaven is a compound made up of mineral substances, nor lit up with gas; but I do not attempt to force my opinions into any one's mind, for my opinion does not prove anything, but I can prove just as much as all the ministers in Christendom, which is just nothing at all, because their arguments are only theoretical, and they cannot locate either of the worlds that they profess to know all about. But, as Dr. McKnight said just before he died, "it is a leap in the dark," and that remark is yet good yet to the living. There are so many misguided minds in the world, that perhaps scare-crow religion does prevent crime in some cases, but it also produces insanity in hundreds of cases.

I think we have thirty-five Lunatic Asylums in the United States at the present time, besides some more in contemplation, and the more I see of the world the more I think as the Doctors did in the Utica Asylum in one respect, which was that about three-quarters of the whole world was crazy on some subject or other; and I very often see people that I consider monomaniacs on different points, and that is one grade of insanity, but they do not know it; as soon as one alludes to that particular point that they are insane upon, they will be excited. Delusions of different kinds generally follow nervous diseases, and in many cases, if the imagination can be reached, it will effect a cure; and I have experimented on some cases in the Asylum, finding it had a very good effect; but I always got up something very ridiculous, indeed, and something that was entirely unexpected to them. If you can get them to laugh natural, it is quite apt to explode the whole affair; and they will yield their indigo feelings because the ridiculous impression is the strongest;—if one can evaporate the old blue dye, the cure is effectual, and a trifle of mirthfulness is very often a great medicine.

But, thank God, the cloud that has hung over the mental horizon is now fast breaking away, and the time is not far distant when the human brain will be allowed the privilege of expanding to its utmost capacity. God never made a peck of brain to be crammed into a pint bowl;—and there are some persons that have had to have their skulls sawed open and a piece of gold inserted, to make room for the brain to do its office. The world is large enough to hold all the brain that there is in it, but the house that the mind lives in is kept locked up, and mamma has got the key; and if bub or sis can think of things that mamma cannot, she tells them not to ask questions—it's wicked to ask such questions. How do children know what disposal to make of their energies of character?—And it is lamentable to see the millions of undeveloped minds that there are in the world; but the Bible government is, "spare the rod and spoil the child," and the mother develops the bumps with sticks and knocks, and rough language, and then two or three times each day she prays to God and tells him all of her own faults and her children's, and asks him to forgive them, just as though he was going to accommodate himself to all the old women's whims in creation.

When I was in the Asylum, they kept me in the basement about six weeks, which was the worst hall in the house, and during the time that I spent there I had what I call a concussion of the brain. It was the greatest state of physical suffering that could possibly be endured, and I feel the effects of it now at times, but I cannot describe the sensation, but I know the cause of it, and it appears to be exactly in the centre of my head. It is a fine noise like two sharp bones grating together. Sometimes I can feel it much plainer than at others, and then perhaps I will not hear from them again in some time. It's not very pleasant to have that little racket in the skull, but perhaps my bump of firmness or self-esteem caved in, and if so, no wonder they made a racket; I presume they are trying to get back again, and after getting up a piece, fall back; I should think the bumps that I have left would begin to fit Syracuse by this time, for in selling my books I was in every public block from the basement to the attic, and some of them were rather low in the wall, and I presume that my veneration is no larger than when I commenced selling books; for it's a knock on one side and a rap on the other until I feel as though some parts of my head had rather caved in. I suppose there will a new set of phrenological developments grow out, and if so, I shall be able to raise a new crop of ideas; and who knows but what they will be a complete fit for Syracuse, and the pious people, and the ministers, and the gossips, and the fashions? If all this should be brought to pass, my last twenty years experience might pay me very well, as far as money would go to pay for mental suffering.

The soil and climate of Syracuse has never been prolific of many great intellects as yet; but I live in hopes that at some future period there will be a few there that will know the difference between good common sense and insanity, and not take a person by storm and pitch them into a Lunatic Asylum with five hundred crazy people. "O consistency, thou art a jewel." Church-going fire-eaters are governed altogether by their feelings;—but there appears to be an unseen agency about to establish a new era, and if so, we shall get religion in a more condensed form. Jesus Christ could concentrate his powers of mind, and he made every word, thought, and action tell. He never launched off into eloquent strains of language without ideas, to make himself fashionable; but he clothed his ideas in very simple language, and he was very dignified but severe in his reproof, courteous in his council, and during his life he was known to smile once and to weep once. But I have done worse than that; for as ridiculous as this old world is now, I should have to carry glue with me all the time to glue my mouth together, if I should make an effort to live without laughing; for my mirthfulness has been my best medicine; and I kept myself alive by the use of it. While in the Asylum, when the Doctors thought they had got me in a tight place, laughing was the only outlet to the feelings; but I now feel as the lion did when he was kicked by the jack, for pop-guns and shot-guns, and long tongues have not taken effect to amount to much, or not so much but what I can wear them out, which they cannot me, and I still choose my own position.

George Washington's mother told him when a child, that if he ever expected to learn to command, he must first learn to obey; and he did so; and if a person starts aright in the world, and continues to pursue that course, they will rise in the world. The only true way is to remove the greatest obstacles on the first start, and if a person can use their character to any advantage, they have a right to, for what is morally just to one's self is equally so to the world, and that is a mutual benefit that never can be obliterated, for every action has its reaction, and if one's course is downward, they will go down to their own place eventually. But I never felt injured by what people said about me;—it was their direct treatment to me; for I had no home nor money, either; and that is the time to try souls; for no person ever knew what the world was, or what it is, until adversity shows them;— but adversity makes the true man, and prosperity makes the monster. People grow into conditions gradually, without realizing how they appear to the world. But Robert Burns said, "If we could see ourselves as others see us, it would from many a trouble free us." And I presume that is one of my own weak points, for a great many have been wise enough to offer their advice free of charge; and I thought that was their weakness, for when

I thought I needed advice, I always went to those that knew more than I did myself.

After I left the Institution, I met a Physician's wife, and she was interested in the case more to gratify her curiosity than to show her humanity; she was very quizzy, and asked me if there was no remedy for my nervous affection. I told her I thought there was, but not in medicine. She said I could have just as much medicine as I wished free of any charge, if I would take it. I told her I did not want to make a medicine-chest of my stomach, but if her husband could make those little white pills reach the petticoat telegraph company, and regulate their treatment to me, my nerves would regulate themselves. As soon as I found that the sale of my pamphlet would secure me a living, I began to feel better; for so far I have been out of their reach, and what they say about me is no more than a July frost. My physical health is perfectly good, and my head is about as good as new; and on the whole I think there is no great loss without some small gain; and perhaps I shall get rational yet. I felt as though my other pamphlet was written on a subject that richly merited public patronage, for it was made up of a class of facts that I know to be true, and that is not all;—the same facts will never be known except it's by the patients, and not by all of them, for they do not all witness them. They must go on to the worst halls to get the whole, and spend a long time there, too.

In a small village in this State I sold a copy of my work to a young lawyer, and I saw at once that he was interested. He asked me if I thought the Asylum to be a moral Institution. I told him that I thought it as much so as any one of the kind. He then told me he had an acquaintance who was a Physician in a Lunatic Asylum, and he had told him a great many facts that he said never was known to the world, which if they were, the Institution would not stand long. I told him that if those walls could talk, they would tell great tales; and if all could be known, they would think my other work gave a very modest description of the house.

But it was fun for me to see Dr. Benedict lock up a

patient because they would get mad, and he could not control himself. He would fly mad just like an old hornet, and once he flew at me and pushed me along a short distance, and I thought I should take my own time and way to get revenge on the gentleman, when they got me into the worst hall in the house. I then took my time to pay all my old debts. In the basement they dish out the food to the patients before they are seated at the table, and the meat, pudding, pie, and gravy, all go on to the same plate. One day after the dinner was dished out, and before we took our seats at the table, who should favor us with a call but the *Hon.* Dr. Benedict, and I then seized on the opportunity to settle with the Doctor. He had on a very fine suit of black cloth, and I took my dinner-plate and threw it at him with some little force, if I am not mistaken. He stood facing me, or as the Irish say, "forninst me"; it took him near the shoulder, and the plate was in pieces too numerous to mention—his coat was a coat of many colors, and his pants showed what kind of gravy we had for dinner. He got Mrs. Maloy, the attendant, to go into the clothes-press with him, and take a knife and scrape off a plate-full of gravy before he cared to pass through the halls; but that job afforded the patients a good dish of fun, and myself a bit of pleasure with the rest. I presume the Doctor thought

"Each pleasure has its poison, too,
And every sweet a snare."

I wish that all the ministers in the world could be in an Insane Asylum for one year, and they would see the effect of Protracted Meetings staring them in the face on every side. The first winter I was there they received eleven patients during five days in one week, and the house was crowded before to its utmost capacity. The only move that could be made was to start a few loads off to the different Poor-houses, but those that were the most benefit to the house they would allow to remain as long as they could, and very often to the injury of the patient. They were very apt to get rid of such as made

them the most trouble as soon as possible. I found that
out by observation; and I was not a very dull scholar in
that department. I had the most of my fun in the fine
ironing room. I liked the girls in that room very well;
and when I wanted to burlesque the Dr.'s government over
me, I always managed to get down into the fine ironing
room, and nothing suited the girls better than to get me
down there and play up insanity, to get the Doctors to
threaten me, and tell what they all said; and many of the
attendants thought me a very fortunate patient, for they
said I could be rational any time I chose  But they often
wondered how I could bear as much impudence from the
doctors as I did; but I knew they employed every effort
to provoke me, and that is the time that I should feel above
getting out of patience with low-bred people. "He that
ruleth his spirit is greater than he that taketh a city." I
know I have struck a vein of egotism, but the world is
more capable of appreciating my bad qualities than the
few good ones that I possess. The gossips will naturally
insinuate a person's reputation away; but they take the
stars that shine the most or the brightest, they never take
an ordinary mind for a bridle to their tongues, for they will
not last long, but they take such as have native character
enough to keep up a sensation; they always select a hobby
from that class. But my character is in my own keeping,
and my reputation is in the hands of the public, and I do
not think strange that it has become partially deranged in
the present state of society. The first low insinuation
that reached my ears after I went to Syracuse, was made
by one of the girls that worked in the shop with myself.
She found out that I had a friend, and she went there and
planted a thorn to rise up and prick her; and she raised a
good crop of thorns. But it was not long before she expe-
rienced religion, and united with the Presbyterian Church,
and she lives in the place yet. Enough of those long
tongues is equal to a cactus hedge, such as they have in
some of the Southern States; they are full of long thistles
on every side. "But we read of a time when all old things
shall be done away;" and I see that old Institutions and old
  ystems of all kinds and classes have yet to have a general

breaking up; but I think it proper to allow all classes of evils to wear out; but the most of reformers are too rabid, they create ten in the effort to obliterate one. But my own history shows forth the effect of a great combination of causes that are still slumbering in their infancy, but God is now asking for a full developement of hidden mysteries, that to the stranger have laid in ambush. But as Mr. Beecher said of the tongue, "they will sting;" and Washington Irving said, "there was no instrument that grew sharper by constant use except a woman's tongue." And there is the foundation of all my insanity. I have been stung with the tongue rather too much, and obliged to bear it, for I had not the means to place myself out of their reach, and I considered their treatment to me a species of insanity, for there are thousands of people in Syracuse who are monomaniacs on that one point, if no other, and eventually it will pass off in the form of an epidemic. But how can they bear the reaction? Sudden transitions are not conducive to health or happiness; but I presume they will be able to find a substitute.

But I feel complimented to know that I have the good will of hundreds that I can neither respect nor associate with; but I love them, and not their faults. I often hear the vulgar remark that such a man is a great loafer; but it takes a great man to make a great loafer; and if the feelings of that class could be reached, we should get a history worth knowing. And so it is with woman; we little know the talent that is running at random in the female department of life, neither can the evils they create be measured, for they will prey upon society to gratify their revengeful feelings, and their influence is felt in every avenue in the social condition of life. But a great many of them are the most high minded beings on earth, but they were not located aright, and all wrecks of mind are only victims of circumstances, and I had much rather go to them for a favor than the most of Church members; I have had favors of both, and I never received an abrupt word from the class that do not claim a standing in society.

But there is another class that prey upon society that are equally as vicious as the other class, but they are very intimate, and many of them have very large secretiveness, and they are so velvety, and the velvet tongues are the ones that make insinuations; and they first make each one promise to keep all a profound secret, for they want the privilege of telling it to each one themselves, and at first, a victim knows he or she is robbed of their reputation. But a great fault with parents is, that they do not establish business habits in their children, and they go out into the world without knowing where to begin life, and they do not fix upon a motive to live for, and no one cares for them only to rob them. And I am not surprised at the present state of affairs, for what inducement is there for one to be morally just, who are thrown upon their own resources, to struggle with poverty and with the other ills of life, for those who give tone to society are determined not to be equaled but only imitated; for I have seen that fact verified, and I have also seen their own works follow them, for sometimes people are so afraid that they should not accomplish what they desire to, that they overdo the business and commit themselves. I have seen a great many cases of that kind and I shall see a few more yet, and I am perfectly satisfied with the result, so far.

But no one knows the sleepless nights that I have passed in Syracuse, and my mind was never idle, and I have a history that the world is yet a stranger to; but we are told not to "cast pearls before swine." And when I thought proper to analyze society, I had to think all night and sew all day; for I worked on the best of goods, and I was obliged to allow fashion and gossip to absorb all my attention during the day, and the worst of all was I could not tell them what I thought of them. Gossip will do for talk but not for thought, and I could not act against influences that were acting around me and against my feelings, and my brain would not allow such a condition of affairs, and I became misanthropic, but a change of circumstances has worn that out, and I have had to help create a set of circumstances that I could live in. And I have had my own weak points to bear, and I have had to bear the weak points of all Syracuse, and the infirmities of the Insane Asylum, doctors and patients, and all the attendants, and I have just sense enough left to get a living by publishing the foolishness of those who have called me crazy. We never know our mental resources until circumstances develope them. Money aristocracy has no charms for me, but useful intelligence and true merit alone is wealth in my eye; I venerate them.

The State of Vermont is a rough corner of creation, and I think perhaps it was made of the fragments of all the rest, and it would not be strange if God finished it up on Saturday night after dark, for it certainly looks like an unfinished job. But nevertheless, a monotonous country always produces some great intellects, and New England affords a class of men that are just fitted to develope the resources of a country and all countries. But if the May Flower had landed in the Western States, the Yankee Land would have been a wilderness to-day. But the most of the old Puritan class were descendants from some of the best English blood in the world, for soon after America was discovered the English unlocked their prison doors and shipped their convicts here to settle up the new world, and by so doing we got the mental aristocracy of England, such as would not bear oppression, for a great many of them were in prison for making some trivial remark about the King, or some other great nuisance such as an intellectual man would not like to be be governed by. And what is there to prevent the Yankees from being first and foremost in investigating principles. I do not wonder the English are proud of us when we do right, for we are only a branch from the English nation, about the same as grand-children.

Since I have been in Canada I feel proud of my ancestry, for there I found a very fine class of English. But not many of the genuine come into the United States, but now and then one; but the most who come here are bogus, just the kind they do not want there. I told them we had got nearly all the foreign rubbish here. They said they knew it; but they were very glad to get rid of the law Irish. But there is very good Irish people in Canada, and they are ashamed of the low Irish. But in England low is law; and it is not to be bought and sold for a few shillings to accommodate every fashionable villain on earth. And the lower classes dread to be chastised by John Bull, and they flee to the land of freedom, where they are hired to vote for a drink of whisky; and they are as ignorant of the politics of this country as a drove of swine. And their influence is not called in question in Canada, and should not be anywhere until there is a great moral change in them; and that will not be very soon, for they are very much afraid of knowing something besides what the minister tells them. But in a very few generations there will be a great change in the lower class of Irish; for those that are born here rather like to be called Americans; but yet they are very treacherous to us. And the most that have come to America have been sent here as paupers by the different parishes. And the Americans passed a law that they should not land on the American shore unless they were furnished with one dollar; and they will come here and go right to the poor-house to be supported on the strength of one dollar. And if the most of them get one dollar after they get here, they imagine that all God's creation is theirs, and they begin to put on their airs.

When I sold books in Buffalo, I went into a Justice's office, and there was two men in the office, and I presented my book to the Justice. And after I had told him what the work was, the other man spoke, and said he, "that book is all a pack of lies." And I asked him what authority he had for saying what he did not know anything about, he said he knew it to be so, for he had seen the book. I told him I had seen the facts that were in the book. I then told him that I presumed that he belonged to the low class of Irish—and I was right. And he told me that if I did not leave off selling those books he would have me arrested, and he told the Justice to make out a warrant, I think he called it. I told him I should wait there and save them the trouble of looking after me; but I did not see the warrant. I was told that he was City Attorney, and as great a villain as he knew how to be; and I knew that without being told. And I told him what he was and what all the low Irish were, and he became passive in a short time. I think he found my remarks were true, whether the book was or not.

After I had sold three editions of my pamphlet, some felt rather disturbed because I found sale for them. And with the rest, I found the Standard Office was in trouble for fear I should get a living as well as themselves. But they are Irish, and it is no wonder they were ashamed of the truth, but I did not suppose their sympathies were with the lower classes; but by reading a short paragraph in the Standard I found I was mistaken. And here it is:

Miss Phebe Davis is getting out her fourth edition of wonderful revelations about the Utica Lunatic Asylum. The extensive sale of her work proves that there are more lunatics out of the Asylum than inside of it.

The wonderful revelations alluded to was an exposition of the treatment that we received from the low class of Irish that were employed there as attendants. I have seen Irish attendants there with live stock in their heads. And there were Irish patients sent there with their heads in such a condition that the doctors furnished the same remedy that farmers use for their cattle. Combs were not fast enough for so numerous a nation as their heads furnished. The Irish cannot bear promotion, they appear to be out of their own latitude.

I was West with my books, and I stopped at a small village, and the agent at the depot was an Irishman, and he told me a falsehood, and I told him of it. And when I went to the depot to take the cars, he took that time to show his impudence; and every man and boy that was around about the time the train was due, he met them at the door and made his low insinuations to them, and they would go in and look around and walk out again. But I knew the game he was playing all the time, but kept still. And at length there was a gentleman appeared, from Manlius, that knew me, and he bought one of my books of me when they were first printed. And as soon as Mr. Irishman commenced his blarny with him, he asked him my business, and he told them all that he knew me very well. And there was a very sudden change in the atmosphere all at once, and the Irishman looked as if a spoonful of dirt would cover him. He was not ashamed of what he had done and said, but to find himself caught in his villainous motives, in the presence of a large number. It is true I did not feel slandered by a low Irishman, but my position was not a very pleasant one among strangers.

I have been very well acquainted with the character of the low Irish, and there is one curious trait in their character, which is, to shape every effort to injure the American whenever and wherever they can. That seems to be the most exalted motive that they live for, and yet they all say that they like the Yankees the best of any people in the world. But I would prefer the Southern Africans, if I could select for myself, for some of them have native character, and one can mould them into men; but an Irishman is destitute of the elements of a man, with the exception of a few individuals. It is true I have seen a very few that were fine men, and that class I respect very much. Burns said "a man was a man for all that,"—and a man is no less a man because he is a native of Ireland; but since America has been converted into a poor-house for the reception of foreign paupers, I think we are entitled to as much as civility from the lower classes.

But low foreign influences have done very much to contaminate the morals of Americans, and I would have the country beware of Catholicism, for it is a dangerous ingredient in the brotherhood of mankind. Although I am no politician, I am doubly interested in the welfare and prosperity of the United States, for my ancestry would all meet a cannon ball half way for their liberty. And I had two brothers in the last war, and they were both in the battle of Lake Champlain, in the year eighteen hundred and fourteen. And when I saw that ground that was once stained with human blood, my devotional feelings were rather active, for I considered it a piece of consecrated earth, bought by the sword, not by great numbers but by united efforts; when America could boast of true men, who made their efforts tell. But now vulgar fashions have taken the place of stern realities, and we must all pray fashionable and even laugh fashionable. And some think it a sin to laugh during the Sabbath day, but no sin connected with all classes of crimes six days of the week. But one day they will all listen to a long, dry, stereotyped prayer, that will evaporate in particles of sulphur long before it gets out of the church door; but no matter for that, if they pay the minister well, for they all treat God as though he was a mute, and had lost his vision too. Mr. Beecher says he does not like to hear people pray cream and live skim milk; But I think they pray ice-cream and live on new milk themselves.

A few years since I got rather short of funds, and I told some of the pious people of it, and one Saint told me to go to God. And it was news to me that Deity dealt in the articles that we happened to need the most when we get hungry; and I told them I could not find the way into his cellar nor pantry. They told me to pray, and I did, but not in a fashionable way. I took a sheet of paper and wrote my prayer, and thanked God for past favors, if they were small, and told him just what I had and just what I needed, and took my prayer to a printing office and got it printed, and sold about eight dollars worth, and that made me very comfortably off for the time being. But the pious people were angry because I had told God the truth, and I think I must have made a cream prayer for the first time in my life, for I never could make any other kind of a prayer that paid well; but I presume I live skim milk with the rest. But I think it is about time to commence telling Deity the truth; for there is an unseen agency lending an influence outside of self interest, and if it is a principle it will cover a great deal of ground, and if deception, it is a work of great magnitude. "But truth is mighty and will prevail." But spirit mediums say that I am and always was an impressive medium, and that I am doubly impressable and must go by my impressions, and I should do aright. And when I do obey my impressions the pious people call me crazy, and I found it necessary to cultivate self reliance, and individualize myself.

I wish to be generous in my feelings, for I am sure I am too illiterate to judge of the truth of the principle that is called spirituality, but I have seen demonstrations that I cannot account for. And I have asked if it was right that I should go to the Insane Asylum, and they say not; but it was the ignorance of the people, that I lived in advance of the age. But the Utica Asylum, nor their discipline nor their medicine did not cure my disease.

After I left the Asylum I was in a family for some time. And at first the woman was very amiable; but she was one of the fitty kind of women, and one day she went into a silent fit or spasm, and threw herself about strangely for awhile, and I did not know but we should get communications from rapping mediums, but she soon passed into the clairvoyant state, and I looked for great revelations out of her long absence of speech. But I saw that her tongue was paralyzed, and I left her. But she recovered from the trance state, and I found that it was not for my especial benefit that she left this sphere. But at first I looked for medical prescriptions, but her mediumship did not fit my insanity. But she is not the first case of the kind that I have seen, and I do not wonder that my nerves are a little crazy at the end of twenty-six years experience in such refined society as Syracuse affords. There is one family in the place that owe me four or five dollars, and have twenty years, for fashionable dress-making. And two of the pinks are dead, that I fixed up finery for, but the old dahlia is yet on terra firma, and when I have asked them for my pay the old man and woman both would answer me by telling me that I was crazy. I told them that I thought crazy folks needed what they worked for as much as rational people. But they are now reaping what they have sown. The old man and his son have both been to the Lunatic Asylum as patients, and their fashionable house has been sold; and the highest object of life with the old man is to follow the railroad track up and down, about the time there is a train of cars due, to get a job of either taking off a limb or putting one on. As he is a surgeon he can make it rather profitable business to find a hand, or an arm, or a head on the track, and the first man that he meets who has the most money, he glues on all the different parts he has had the good luck to find, whether they belong to him or not; and as soon as the job is completed he starts for his office to make out his bill, and his charges are always to the extent of the man's purse.

I have heard folks tell of the "grab game," and I know it is rather a vulgar phrase, but I think it must fit the case I have alluded to, if it will anywhere.

I hope I shall not intrude upon the patience of my friends by wishing them to read my history; but as I have been made a conspicuous subject of interest so long, without my consent, I hope they will please to have the patience to read it, or a small portion of it, for I have had to have any amount to bear it all. And the most of it, or the most contemptible part, cannot be described, for no language can reach the intricate meanness of the lower classes.

One woman told me that she had often visited the grave-yard, and that she had met others there that had friends buried beneath the green sod, and they sympathized with each other, and made calls of condolence, and mingled their tears with each other, and set forth the good qualities of their dead friends. And each one would take a few beautiful flowers to plant on the graves of their friends, and watered them with their tears. And the separation must have been painful in the extreme; for when they were obliged to separate, the benediction was pronounced by asking each other if they knew where crazy Miss Davis was. And their oratorial powers were called out, and there was no more weeping till they met again. As their tongues grew lively their tears dried up, and they would like to know what the tormented critter was up to, and who would have her about; and some of the crowd never failed to lock their doors when they saw the crazy, ugly thing coming. I suppose this is grave-yard solemnity, but I never asked that party for information; it has been forced into my brain voluntarily on their part.

It appears my crazy reputation has brought me before the world as rather of a prelude; and in sewing societies I find that it is used more as an interlude. And I am always happy to be remembered, especially in my absence. But this class have no moral courage, just one look from a positive mind will silence an army of the same class.

## CHAPTER III.

There is a kind of brute bravery in this world that is destined to exterminate. Although Napoleon Bonapart was considered a great man, yet he was one of that class of men. And so was Alexander the Great another of those superior men of the age in which he lived, but after he had subdued the whole world, he wept because there were no more worlds to conquer. But the base of their brain predominated, and their feelings over reached their better judgement, because their brain was not well balanced. And all disturbers of the peace, both great and small, belong to the same class. But tattling women are only the refuse, and the tendency is to exterminate; but they never reflect, for the only motive is to fan up the flame of discord. Their influence reminds me of a Canada thistle in a windy day. After the seed is well ripened it is very light, and the wind takes it in every direction, and wherever it locates it will take root and bring forth in a tenfold proportion. And it is just the case with all classes of tattlers. Their tongues are a two-edged sword, and the sword obliterates, but the pen perpetuates. "Facts are stubborn things, and truth is eternal as the heavens." But we are creatures of circumstances and conditions, both previous to our birth and all our lives, but there is only the few that know their destiny is fixed previous to their birth; but observation will teach one the fact, and it is a very important fact, too.

In some portions of Europe they were obliged to regulate the social condition of the lower classes by legal authority, for there were so many imperfect children that pauperism became too great a burden, and the authorities observed the cause of it, and they took thousands out of dismal and dark cellars and old hovels for the purpose of improving the race, and what they send here look as though they could make greater improvement than they ever have. And Americans can do very much to improve the condition of the poor, every way, but our own poor are neglected because foreign pauperism uses all the public funds; and if a respectable American is unfortunate, and needs assistance, they cannot be assisted, for the low Irish cattle must be supported, for their vote is wanted to keep a class of worthless fellows in office. And the most of them are drunk three quarters of their time, and many a poor widow woman earns money to pay her taxes when she ought to be asleep. And at the same time, men who are employed to fill responsible positions are supporting every habit of dissipation at her expense, or at the expense of those in similar circumstances; and I hope there will be a time when women will be able to protect themselves.

But there is one interesting specimen of the female race in Syracuse, she lives on Elizabeth street, and I presume she will start a reformation, for she belongs to the graveyard association, and she must have a very etherial nature, for she looks just like a half grown cat-fish. Her domestic fowls, such as hens, are more companionable for her than ladies society is; for when she lost one old shanghai she was a sincere mourner, much more so than when her son died, for she said the shanghai laid every day, and she could get one more cent per dozen for her eggs than she could for the old speckled hen's, because they measured one size larger. Her house looks like a huge pile of old flood wood after a severe freshet, and her acquisitiveness is so very large that she will go out and gather up and horde all the old clothes and all the old rags, and every part of her house looks like the refuse of a paper mill. Her greatest trouble is about the murders that I have always been going to commit.

When I compare the inferior class of women that Syracuse affords with the great noble wrecks of mind that I saw in the Lunatic Asylum, I feel as though the world was a cypher without them, or their influence, as a guide-board for the minor class. There was Miss Elizabeth Whitning, who has been there for seventeen or eighteen years, who fitted two or three of her brothers for college previous to her going there. She is the greatest genius that I ever saw. Mr. Fowler said that she had constructiveness enough to build a steamboat; but her talent is lost to the world, she is a life patient, but it takes a rogue to cheat her in a bargain now. She is as bright as steel, and she worshipped in spirit and in truth. She was a particular friend of mine, and I was proud of her acquaintance, for I could always learn something from her every day. My seat at the table was next to her, and she always asked God to bless our meals; and I often told her that she would have to bless some of it a long time to make it eatable, and she generally did. She was quite fond of butter, and some of the patients were apt to help themselves to rather more than than their part, and she knew that, and she would pray with one eye open, or open them both and take a look at what she liked best, and if the butter was going rapidly she would reach over and get her part. I often reminded her of the condition of the provision on the table, and she would thank me and go along with her blessing.

I find that an active nervous temperament that is full of thought and intellect want full scope to dispose of their energy, for if not they will become extremely excitable. Such a mind cannot bear a tight place, and that is one great reason why women are much more excitable than men, for their minds are more active; but they must be kept in a nut-shell because they are women. An active temperament generates what I call a surplus of thought, because one cannot dispose of ideas as fast as they coin them. Society compels them to make their mouth a sealed book, for you must consult fashion at the expense of your reason.

We often see a wire muzzle on the canine nose when the hydrophobia becomes an epidemic; and for all we claim freedom of speech, our mouths are subjected to monarchial government just as much as the dogs are to the muzzle. There is one old fact that I would like to have die out, which is, that a woman must not speak a loud word because St. Paul said that they must not. What if he did say so, he was only one man in the world, and that was only his opinion; and who cares for the opinion of one love sick old bachelor, after he has been dead for conturies.

But the men have always kept the women just where old St. Paul left them. He could not get the lady that he thought the most of, and of course he disliked the women. From that circumstance it has become an established fact in the eyes of the world at large, that a woman must not express her opinion on a subject of any importance; but they are beginning to cut loose from the old straight jackets, and the men will be obliged to yield to their influence. Old tyrants squirm a little, but the genuine gentlemen appreciate their motives. I would like to see them all claim their individual rights, independent of organized societies; but it appears necessary to fix upon a starting point by resorting to measures that will bring the subject before the public, and allow the women to establish claims to their rights, for they have got to be educated to know what their proper rights are. But right is right, and right wrongs no man; but I presume I never shall convulse the world with my feeble arguments in favor of women's rights, for I have been imprisoned over two years simply because I presumed to claim my individual rights. That job was a lesson to me; for I found out how inefficient men were in appropriating means. The ignoramuses who invented the plot of my being taken to the Asylum, were a weak class of men, and as crazy as I was. I thought they were standing in their own light all the time; but "they chose darkness rather than light, because their deeds were evils." It appeared to me that I could see where they were blind, for the course that I was pursuing looked right to me, and I thought I could see the result operating in my favor just as plain as I could see my face by looking in a mirror. I suppose they will be obliged to fall back upon their own folly and allow me to pass along in my own way; their means never justified their plans, they had more mouth than brains. Doesticks said that "some have a mouth large enough for a railroad depot;" and there is one now on Clinton street who uses her mouth for a store-house, and she could establish a livery stable in the front part of it if she had a small capital to start with. But there would be one great trouble in her case, she could not keep it locked, for her tongue would pick any lock in the United States. She has waded through seas of tribulation for fear her reputation would suffer by false reports; and what a pity it is that the little frail, delicate, sensitive plant should suffer by the ills of life. The sylph-like form and siren voice, together with her native grace, are a class of accomplishments that will receive the respect of the first class wherever she is known. But it requires first class language to set forth her superior qualities of mind, and I find it rather dry business for me to write out her history.

One of the crazy women in the Asylum said there was fun in fools sometimes, and I have seen the truth of the remark verified in a few instances.

Not long after I left the Asylum there was a lecture given out in the daily papers, and I boarded some distance from the heart of the city, but was not afraid to go alone, and chose to go alone rather than to try to put on fashionable extras; for I knew that I was as good as the rest were at home, and I chose to act natural, and I knew that their out-door appearance was superficial. Two or three of the would-be-ladies met to hold a council to know whether it was best to allow me to go to the lecture with them or not. The jury were out some time, and at length the verdict was given, not; but how to manage to get the job off of their hands was the most profound consideration in the case. Finally it took four to mature the plan; they all agreed to go very early, and while they were engaged in that profitable job, I was washing and ironing my clothes to prepare myself to write my other book to try to get a living. Intricate plans were nothing to me, no more than the news of the boy's father's death was to the boy, as the story goes: some one told a boy that his father was dead, and he told them that was nothing to him, and passed along. I never have time to pay attention to what the women say about me, but some of the crowd generally tell the news. But the said lecture was all over long before I heard of their plans, and I had not thought of wishing to go with them; and I derived a benefit by being told of it, for I had struck a small vein of the blues, and on hearing the plot it ran over the blue streak to reach the organ of mirthfulness, and I enjoyed a good hearty laugh and all was aright. That is only one circumstance out of hundreds of similar ones. The idea was, they thought I should learn as much as themselves; and I should be afraid to go alone, and if they went off and left me, I should lose what they would gain. But if I happen to see or meet any of them when they are arranging a plan to operate against me, I can tell by their looks what they are about; but I do not take any notice of them, nor let them know that I can read them. After a while some one of the party will tell of it, but if they treat me well in my presence it is all I ask; and if they do not, it is their job, not mine, until I want to write a book, and then it is a very small portion of my capital; it is a cheap kind of every day spice.

When my pamphlet was in type in the Chronicle office, Mr. Clark told me there was more than forty persons ran to his office to tell him not to publish it, for he would not get his pay for the job. I asked him who they were, and he said the most of them were Unitarians, and men at that; but he did not tell me of it until I went and paid him forty dollars, in a short time, too. I had paid for one edition before, and I only got nine hundred copies of the first, and paid all of twenty or thirty dollars more than I ought to; but I found Mr. Clark very honorable in his charges. I thought men were engaged in very small business, yet "it is human to err but divine to forgive."

I write these facts to show up human nature just as I have found it, and I wish that some person would take a version from my other pamphlet and this one together, and dramatize them, and I believe they might pay well in a theatre, if different characters could be well represented.

But we are all sure of one place that will remind us of a Quaker meeting; it is the grave-yard. A great many of the class that I have alluded to are now resting in the shell, and perhaps a great many of the class that I have murdered are now holding their heads on with their hands, or perhaps they have a sticking plaster in the spirit world to stick heads on with. I hope they will be sure and stick **the right ones together,** for mistakes of that kind would be very laughable in public. If one should happen to be rather moody a figure of that kind, might reach the mirthfulness and brush away the hallucination at once.

A patient in the Asylum was in despair because she thought her soul was mortgaged to the clerk of the other world, to pay the debt of original sin, and she looked as solemn as a funeral procession. I asked her what she was feeling bad about, and at first she drew a long breath. I followed her feelings, and I found the delusion was riveted in her mind as firm as an old sailor's chest was ever dovetailed together. She imparted her feelings to all whom she met, and I asked her how she knew that she should be lost; she said because she knew it would be the case. I told her that was no argument, it was all in her feelings, that they could make a better use of fuel in this age of railroad speed, and sulphur had a medicinal quality in it that was very valuable, and there was another fact connected with the affair; she began to look at me, and I found I had made an impression. I then told her that there was no conveyance running in that direction, and that the old place was full, and they had closed the doors to allow the fire to go out and cool down. The woman laughed, and it broke the spell, and she got well and went home.

I think I could have done good there if the Doctors had treated me well; but I must be treated like a crazy person whether I was crazy or not. There was a chapel in the house, and Mr. Goodrich was our Doctor of Divinity, or spiritual guide, and every Sabbath that I heard him preach he told God the condition of the unfortunate class that were present, that he had seen fit to afflict, and asked him to restore them to their reason. I thought that to accuse God of creating that condition of things, was wholesale slander in the sight of Deity. I presume the minister meant well, but I thought God did not do much for us, not quite as much as he ought to have done, seeing that he had got us all in a tight place, where we could do nothing for ourselves. But I hope they will please to pay me what they stole from me while I was there.

In selling my other book, I found a great many people that appeared to know that they were very apt to take things that did not belong to them, and from the office, as well as in the halls. There are so many that carry valuables there, that one person could clear a very handsome salary by stealing the deposits of that office. When I present my bill to the managers of the Institution I shall claim double interest on stolen property, as I was sent away an incurable patient. I thought I could make what little change I had very useful, and I sent to the office for it, but the word was that it was not there. I was as well off as Jesus Christ was when he was on earth, as good as he was; he had no place to sleep, and I left a few things in a family when I went to the Asylum, and they told me I could lodge there. But they were very poor, and I could not expect them to board me; my friends helped me to a few eatables, and I was able to earn a trifle myself. I hung on to life strangely until I could find a place to write my book, and when I had taken it to the printing office, I found a woman who allowed me to work for my board a few weeks. But they were poor, and I left there before they could get my pamphlet out. I did make out to get enough to eat, because Mrs. Grove Lawrence had told me never to go hungry, and when all the rest had locked me out of their houses, I was obliged to go there. I did not like to wear out the friendship of those who were willing to do for me, and had done everything that the rest of the world would not do. They always allowed me a place in their sitting-room to unload my brain and mop the tears out of my eyes; and I have shed tears enough in their house to do all their house cleaning for one year. When I could not sleep anywhere else, I could always get a good night's rest in their house. While the rest were barking my insanity all over creation, they always appeared to know just what to say to me; the law of affinity or intuition appeared to teach them that, without any effort on their part.

Mrs. Charlotte Smith is the first lady who suggested the idea of my making the effort to get a living by writing. But they understood phrenology, and where others were weak they were strong, for they always improved every opportunity of learning all the usefuls. About the time I became acquainted with the family, I was rather inclined to be suicidal, for I could not live on sectarianism, and I was trying to reach up to a platform of philosophical facts, and I had to go by marked trees, and in the forest and fog of all the old theories. I got lost and could not find my way out, and each church claimed to be right. They all said I must locate in the church vicinity; but I did not see fit to hitch my team to their post, because they did not look right to me. I could not see anything to live for until I found one family that looked at things through the same glasses that I did. Yet they could not believe just as I did in every respect, but they thought I was as honest in my opinion as they were in their's, and respected my honesty in expressing my opinions, and that was worth everything to me at that time; it was the healing sanative to my feelings, and sympathy is a great medicine alone. I have now been acquainted with Mrs. Grove Lawrence and her daughter, Mrs. Smith, about nineteen years, and have been in their family more than in any other in Syracuse, and whenever I went there I always learned something that was good and nothing that was bad or wrong. I should be very happy to say that of all my acquaintances in the city, but my conscience is not made of India rubber. It is true I have received many favors from others, but nearly all of them partake of the character of the Spaniard enough to give one a dirk in the back, with the ever raised sharp weapon. That class have no moral courage, for the corrupt never have. If I had taken notice of all that has been told me by the same, that could say anything to fit into any small corner to fill out the programme, Syracuse would have been equal to Mount Vesuvius, and fire engine houses would occupy nearly all the city. I had to gossip a little to secure myself a home, and then I could not always do it. Any other conversation was my insanity, but I was careful not to tell all, and not to commit any; but those who told me the most were those who said the most themselves. I marked the class who told me as a favor, as they said, and I let it go so, for it was a favor to me to know what they were, and see them commit themselves. And now they have all got to die in their own dirt, and a number of the beautiful flowers are already at rest.

I have learned that friendship is based on selfishness. I think there is no true friendship outside of interest, and until three years past I have never believed with Dr. Franklin in that respect. I have learned to do as Hannah Moore recommended all to do, which was to sip the honey from every flower, for censure never has corrected the wrongs of this world, but " charity covers a multitude of sins." But sometimes I am at a loss to know how far one ought to extend their charity, yet I know there are extenuating circumstances in some cases. But there are some cases in Syracuse that I hardly know how to dispose of, and one of them is a family on Warren street. I once asked them to allow me to stay in their house during the night, and the woman said that she had no spare bed. I then told her that I could lodge with the hired girl, and she said the girl had but one pillow on her bed. Before I left the house there was a man and his wife from Auburn called there, and the woman asked them both to stay all night, and I was present and heard her urge them to stop during the night. I left on the strength of that dish of piety. There are three in the family, and all middle aged, and no children, nor they never had, but fast Presbyterians and wealthy people. I have been told that they pray as often as the clock strikes; but the woman once gave me a piece of advice that had the solids in it; for she was positive enough to make an impression. She said there was one very bad doctor in the city, and she cautioned me against speaking to him, or ever making his acquaintance in the world, for he was a very dangerous person. I listened to her arguments for awhile, and then told her that I had been acquainted ten or fifteen years, and had not seen anything of the kind. I told her that I had often been told what an awful man he was, but I could not see how so many found it out. After awhile I learned to notice that all of the class of women who knew so many bad folks were just as bad themselves as they had told me that others were. Those women are the very identical beings who are reaching their tongues around myself, and they are to be dreaded in society. The motive is to talk others down to help themselves up ; but egg shells are poor side walks. True merit will always recommend itself to the virtuous; and the influence of that low, vulgar class is growing less, but rather slow, but thank Heaven for small favors.

I am proud to know that the poor respect me, and all other unfortunate beings are my friends. While in the Asylum, among the rest of my friends was a very interesting lady by the name of Cassada. During the time I was in the hall with her she was more than a mother to me, although she was a patient herself. She did more to make the patients comfortable in the hall where she was, than all the doctors and attendants in the house; but old Em. Sales was provoked at every good act that any one did for a patient. Mrs. Cassada is now dead, but all her good qualities live in her children, or I believe she has but one living, and that is a son, and I heard him spoken very highly of when I sold books in the place where he lives It was between Utica and Albany, but I do not recollect the place; but he was in a bank, and I sold him a book

## CHAPTER IV.

When I left the Asylum I found that the patients thought they had lost a friend, and I knew I had lost more friends there than I had anywhere else in this world. I left some inveterate enemies there, but every one of them will suffer a just fate. After I left I tried to arrange a plan to place myself where I could write my pamphlet, and it was very amusing to listen to the plans that some of the women would strike out for me. One woman who had a large house and a small family, thought it would be a wise plan for me to furnish up an old Irish shanty that Tommy Riley had lived in. It was at the further side or end of the back yard to the dwelling house, and was about the size of a cow shed, or a Western barn that they build for one horse or one horse or one cow, and always throw prairie grass over the slight roof; and they are impervious to the severe storms that visit the prairie country. The woman who advised me to rent the rough board shanty, then lived on West Fayette street, in a large double house, and felt very large; but since that her husband has died, and she has had to do as I do, which is, the best she can. I thought I would remind her of the shanty as an act of kindness.

And there was another woman who looked out a place for me that was a splendid residence; but the great trouble was then, that I had not furniture to furnish the mansion, for it was almost a match to Mr. Longstreet's magnificent dwelling. It was built for a tool house, the man who owned it had a very large garden and a vacant lot, where he raised vegetables, and in the centre of the lot he had put up a small hut, large enough to hold his garden utensils. It was made of rough boards, flat roof, and no windows, and great cracks all around. I do not think that I could stand up in it,—that rough board hut was not even fit for a dog kennel. The woman who belonged to the big house told me that I had better go back to the mad-house again, and I told her that I had been in too many mad-houses already, for I seldom went into a house without finding two or three mad women in it, which made it very agreeable. They generally all quarrel about something, and once or twice I have asked them if they would stop quarreling long enough to allow to rest and get breath. The reply was that they were in their own house and they would do as they liked.

Before I could get my book ready for sale I was obliged to go to the printing office and ask the printer to allow me to stop in the office all night, and he gave me the key and a box of matches, and told me to stay in the office until he got there in the morning, for he did not wish the key left in the door; he went away quite early, and I did as he requested me.

I had not one cent of money, and I could not command a house, and the women would crowd me into places that I should not choose under any other circumstances, and then use the case as a weapon to reach my reputation with. I told them that they knew how I was situated, for I always made my case known to a number of them before going where I was sometimes obliged to. One of the ladies told me, about a year since, that I had lived it down; but it was news to me that I had anything to live down. There is one fact that I am sure of, which is, that they cannot live down their treatment to me; for I in my poverty could not select my own society. I have received a great many favors from the hands of what is called the lowest classes; and our Saviour had to go to the lower classes for protection. He found the upper tens to be the worst class in the world, in his day, and they have all kept their standing, but they are now on slippery ground. I know it is rather hard for fashionable idiots to succumb to the influences of the working class. But progression is hard on the bit, and scientific agriculture is the mainspring in all the pursuits in life, it leads the van.

The aristocracy may now want a new set of prayers stereotyped, for they now give God the credit of all the fast bargains they make, which is only a fashionable apology in the eyes of the ignorant for cheating them handsomely. I think that pious people make a pack horse of the Deity, about the same as the Arabs do of the camel. He is their only beast of burden, and under all circumstances the praying class call on Providence for counsel, and repeat all their misfortunes to Him, and ask His advice in all matters of importance. And yet they all say that He knows all things, and is unchangeable, and I cannot see the use of the long string of advertisements that go up every day, or start to go up; but I presume they lose their efficacy before they get half way there, for words are cheap in these days of plenty. I try to select all the best words I can to put into my book, for I have been told that Providence overruled all my business. But I think as an old woman did in Vermont when her house burned down. Her friends went in to administer a trifle of holy consolation, by telling her that she ought to be reconciled to her misfortunes, for the hand of Providence was in all things, and that it was for her good or special benefit that God worked by means. She listened to their arguments a short time, and she saw there was no money in them, and at last she told them that she did not see what business Providence had with her things, that she worked for before she was married. I hope my insanity will be an apology for all the funny things that I publish, for the Great Spirit tolerates all my proceedings, and that is all I ask.

When I was in the Asylum I saw a concentration of evils in a condensed form; and when I said anything to the Doctors about the wrongs of the house, they would tell me that was my insanity. I told them that a fact was no less a fact because it was told by a crazy person.

I once met a physician in this State who told me that he once had a sister in the Utica Asylum. He said he called to see her, and the Doctors told him that she could never be cured, that she was just as well then as she ever would be. He said at first she hardly noticed him, and appeared very stupid, but he began to talk with her, and after a long time she appeared to wake up a little. He told me that he stayed with her two or three hours, and that he never saw such a change in a person in the same length of time; and he took her home in a few days, and she was then superintending her domestic affairs. He thought if he had not seen her when he did that she would have been idiotic in a few weeks. I told him that I had seen a number of such cases, for there is no interest taken in a great many of them, and the mind ceases to act, it comes to a stand still, and the result is idiocy in many cases.

It requires ingenious people to have the care of the insane to effect cures. Sometimes a very trivial circumstance will restore a person to their reason. They are treated too much like children, and it would be a great help to many if they could be thrown upon their own mental resources more than they are. When they go there they are stripped of every responsibility in the world, and also of every privilege that they have been accustomed to, and the mind is left to become a dead weight on itself; a person in that condition is only a mere cypher. The mind should be kept interested all the time, not by coertion but by persuasion.

When I was South selling my books, I met a lady who had been Matron in a Lunatic Asylum, and she told me that there was a milliner that had been a patient there a long time, and all the doctors said there was no help for her. Nothing would do her any good, and the Matron thought she would experiment on the case. She invited her to walk to the village with her, and look out a piece of silk for a bonnet, and told her that she wanted her to make it, and to do it just as she chose to herself. She did so, and when she had finished the bonnet she was perfectly sane, and in a few weeks she went home to her family.

The great trouble in Lunatic Asylums is, they want to cure them by rule. They have their written rules, and all who cannot be cured by being subjected to their code of laws are pronounced incurable at once; and their rules are enough to make a rational person crazy, for they are almost equal to Fox's Book of Martyrs. I knew when I was there that Doctor Benedict would not be allowed to stay there long, yet his motives were just as good as Dr. Grey's, but they have a different way of showing their motives. Dr. Cook was very much of a gentleman, rather young to be employed in a place where there were minds far superior to his own; but he is capable of improvement, for he had a fine intellect. Dr. Porter knew about as much as all the doctors in the house. I saw a number of his relatives when I sold my books, and I found that he belonged to an intelligent family, such as I call the first class. But there are few physicians who have a good medical talent. Reading books does not always qualify men for eminent physicians. There is no healing qualities in medicine, it only causes the diseased organs of the system to act, but the life and the healing principle is in the person.

I have one compliment to pay to the spiritual theory, or principle as it is called, which is the fact that when I am under the influence of one class of those who call themselves spiritualists, I feel just as well as I ever did in my life, and my nerves are quiet and I can sleep perfectly quiet, and I do not feel confused at all, and all is aright with myself. All those who play up afraid of me, are guilty of some very base wrong, either directly to me or about me. If they have not injured me it is not because they have not tried, or do not intend to try. I am glad they are afraid of me, for they mind their business better than usual. But it is only the guilty that dodge at my presence; where there is no guilt there is no fear. I have seen persons dodge for me, and yet were not above stabbing me with their tongues, and on the whole it is rather amusing for me to see them dodge, and run, and look, and whisper, and say, "there, she is coming." But I do not appear to notice it, and yet I see it all, for they all look just as they feel. They will look well going into Heaven with the same faces that they looked at me with, for many of their faces reminded me of an old dish cloth just after it is wrung out of dirty water, and in a hundred shapes at that. The afraid kind, watch me as close as an old gander used to, that we had when I was a child and lived at home. In the spring, about the time the young goslings appeared, I was rather troublesome to the geese, and the old fellow got rather cross. There was a number of us children, and he had all he could do to attend to us all, and he being of the amphibious family, he wanted to spend a portion of his time in the brook. But he was always on duty, and if he saw one of us going in his direction he would start out of the water and run and fly at us, and report us to the old goose, and they would consult together to know what was best to do. The old fellow actually became goggle-eyed with anxiety; and so have the people of Syracuse, from anxiety, curiosity and fear.

A short time after I left the Asylum I was in the east part of the city, and it appears that a man, or something that claimed to be a man, thought that I needed a lecture. He went into the barn, and a light of glass was broken out, and the first I knew his face was in a frame, talking to me. He had rather a large face, and was a little provoked at the time, and a florid complexion, and on the whole he did not present a very pleasing spectacle. The rage he was in gave his voice anything but a subdued tone, or else I have not a correct ear for music. I listened a short time to his siren-like notes, and I was not charmed into a trance, and I looked at him and told him that he did not look well in a frame and passed along.

I have seen people very angry because they could not provoke me to quarrel with them. One woman would try her best, and when she found that her efforts proved a failure, she would fly into a spasm. I have seen her run with all the fire and fury that an animal nature is possessed of, and take the broom and sweep nearly every griddle off of her cooking stove on to the floor. One would think they were in a blacksmith's shop, if they were blind, instead of a private dwelling house, with a lady who was brought up in high life. And then she was telling around that she was giving me a home; but my home was a perfect bedlam, and I left her and had a long fit of sickness. She was not the only one that was accessory to that. But I lived through it all, and there were many that were very sadly disappointed. My case was enquired after daily, with all the interest in the world; and when I got well and went out, it was fun to see how cross they looked; but I kept still. When I was sick I laughed to myself, thinking what a spicy advertisement or obituary I should get if I happened to go to the field of spirits that time. But "there is a divinity that shapes our ends, rough hew them as we will."

There has been times that I was short of means, and did not feel like going hungry in a land of plenty. I knew that they often took up subscriptions in the different churches for the poor, but I not being a member of any minister's church, they made me an outcast in all the fashionable church crowds, and I thought I would help myself to a few shillings off of the plate as they called around. I never took but fifty cents, just enough to supply my wants for the time being. The act of taking that money threw every church in the place into a perfect simmer. I had ought to go to the mad-house; and they all had a rich time out of four shillings, and every church became a madhouse simply because I did not choose to go hungry.

A year or two before I went to the Asylum I was keeping house, and I did all that I could to provide for myself. It was very warm that summer, and I lived in the house with a tailoress, and often helped her a trifle. I lived plain, and there was a day or two that I had not much to eat except a small bit of dried beef and rather poor bread, and I was doing a job of very hard sewing and had got very tired, and near night I went out and got a trifle to eat. I did not eat very hearty, but it gave me the cramp in my stomach, and I had to send for the doctor in a few hours. After that I thought I was justified in doing as I have, because I thought it morally just to myself, for I could not get it by telling christians that I was in a tight place. An active brain requires very good food, for the wear of the nervous system is such that if the physical demands are not well supplied the brain suffers very soon. The same summer that I was sick there was an epidemic prevailed through the country, and it visited Syracuse, and the people were afraid to eat because they were afraid to die. I had neither of these fears; nothing to fear but a great deal to hope for, because I thought they would give me what they did not want or had no use for, as they were afraid to eat themselves. When I read the daily papers I began to console myself, that then was my harvest, and after reading a number of pious advertisements I started out in pursuit of provisions. But I found myself sadly disappointed in appearances, for although there were some in the weeds of mourning, yet every key was secured, and perhaps in the coffin; and I did not injure my constitution by carrying home what I could get. The cabinet-makers and grave-diggers made money that summer, and I hope the doctors were paid better than I paid mine for the one visit, for I told him that I would pay him when I got rich. I suppose he made no charge on the strength of that promise.

What a time we should have in this world if God should ever put a padlock on to old mother earth. They have got everything else under lock and key now, but it appears they keep open doors there for all to go and some to come back. When I visit the spirit world, I expect to see a panorama of all things in this world, or a true representation in some form or other, and if people are judged there according to their merits here, I am thinking that some of the fashionables will occupy the rear corners. The foolish customs of the age prompts many a man to commit crimes. I presume if Dr. Webster had not have had a fashionable family he would not have taken the life of Dr. Parkman. But his salary was only twelve hundred dollars per annum, and he had fashionable daughters who would not soil their hands with honest labor; but their unfortunate father stained his hands with innocent blood to support his family fashionably. How strange it is that we are led by fashions when we all ought to know what class we are imitating. Paris, in France, leads in fashions, and the same class who lead in fashions lead in vice. I have always thought that God was a Quaker, because he never has been the author of as much as one fashion. But He made man upright, and He has sought out many inventions.'

## CHAPTER V.

I have only second or third class brain to set forth the beauties of mechanism. My descriptive powers are not very active; but I love the beautiful both in nature and in art and science. Man is the moving power of the world. We must acknowledge that the mechanics constitute a very great share of usefulness in almost every avenue of life. Mechanical genius must emanate from Deity, although mechanics are often spoken of by the fashionables, or as I call them, the lower classes, as though they were useless, or some of the lower order of emigrants. Yet the organ of constructiveness must be inherited from God, for God certainly was the first, and the greatest, and the most expeditious mechanic that we have any account of. We worship God as our maker and our preserver, and still allow ourselves to despise his works. Our Saviour was a mechanic, and his mother was a poor working woman, and Joseph was a carpenter by trade, and he was an engraver and sculptor, and by working at them all he gained himself a comfortable living. Jesus often worked with Joseph, but perhaps he was not an independent workman, for he left Joseph and Mary when he was very young. But our Maker and Saviour were both of them mechanics, and of course they belonged to the working class. But just look into the streets on Sabbath mornings and see the running to and fro to worship God and his only begotten Son. But who builds the houses that they all run to every few days but mechanics, and who builds fashionable private dwellings and furnishes them, and who are fashionables beholden to for their fine dress but the mechanics.

When Dr. Franklin first made the attempt to bottle up electricity, they all laughed at the idea. He told them that all men had once been children, there had been a beginning to all things, and yet the majority will use every effort to block up the wheels of progression. I think it is sixty years since Robert Fulton invented the first steamboat, and they made all sorts of fun of him, but the head he wore told him what he could do. The Mississippi River shows that there has once such a man lived as Robert Fulton. All rivers and lakes are dotted with the invention of one man's brain, which is a small institution, but covers a great deal of ground but more water. The first paper manikin that was ever invented was invented by a Frenchman, and he worked on it thirty years, and they called him crazy all the time; but he made a complete job of it, and now who is there who does not like to understand physiology. And nearly every railroad in the United States is fenced in by telegraph wires, and all these benefits are derived from mechanical geniuses, as vulgar as fashionable fools think mechanics are. Just take them out of the world, and I think there will be some blank pages. But they all like to ride on the cars, and I wonder if they could make their own cars and engines, and superintend railroads. We all like to read papers and books, but printing was invented by a mechanic, and even the Holy Bible must come out of the printing office.

I should like to see a fashionable man or woman set types for just one paper and distribute them. I presume they would think that printing was not the vulgar business that it has been represented to be. But the minor class can stand back of the counter and sell ribbons and lace. And yet there are some bright men in dry goods stores, but they are only selling what mechanics have manufactured. Ladies and gentlemen are all beholden to the vulgar mechanics for their finery and good looks. When they look in the glass to admire themselves or their dress, they only admire what the working class have done, but they despise their occupation. Their elegant household furniture that they so much admire, and are so very proud of, does not grow out of the ground in the form of sofas and rocking chairs, and their carpets are not gathered from the trees like apples, neither are their boots and shoes dug out of the ground like a potatoe, nor their fine bonnets and splendid dresses do not grow on corn stalks, but the milliner, and dress maker, and tailor, and shoe maker are rather necessary evils after all that is said about the low class of mechanics. I think that if all classes were obliged to make their own clothes they would prefer a small sized glass to admire themselves in.

Almost any man who has the organ of language well developed, can take what the thinker has said and written and pass it around, and he gets all the credit that a thinker is entitled to, and at the same time he is anything but an intellectual man. There is some difference between words and ideas, as much as there is between philosophy and theory.

Pythagoras lived five hundred years before Christ, and his class of ideas were very similar to Christ's, but the people did not know what he meant, and he could not establish his principles. Neither could Plato, for the people were not susceptible of his teachings. But their philosophy was no less true because the people were illiterate; it is easier to condemn than it is to investigate.

We read of a time when the sheep and the goats shall be separated; and the world is a baby now to what it will be one hundred years hence. Wealth will have less influence, and mind will rule this world eventually, and a person who will wish to live on what others produce will not be thought any more of than a highway robber is now; and there is no difference in reality, or in the sight of God, for one is the vulgar criminal and the other is the legal criminal, or the fashionable criminal.

If I had the ability to set forth all the beauties of mechanism, it would only be an intrusion on the minds of the people to read it, for it would cover ten acres of ground. All the refined class appreciate it now, for it is before their eyes on every side. Even at a fashionable funeral we see the work of a great many first class mechanics, for coffins and shrouds are all fitted up by the vulgar mechanics. But when they are deposited in the cemetery, the rich and the poor are all free soilers alike; and when God takes the census of that hotel he does not ask how much money they left here, but perhaps he will ask some of them how and where they got their money.

There are many little accomplishments in this world

that do not speak very loud for themselves, except to the
close observer. To be a finished seamstress is an accomplishment that but few persons are blessed with. Only a
few years since I heard a literary lady speak of a first class
vest-maker by saying that she was nothing but a sewing
girl. She knew she had married well, and the lady was
poor herself. She knew that I was a dress-maker, and she
made other severe remarks that were not becoming in a
lady to make about one who had never injured her at all.
She said that Thomas Paine's bones had ought to have been
made into buttons long ago. But his death is celebrated in
Boston every year, and not by low, vulgar minds, but by the
intellectual and refined, such as can appreciate what he did
for the political world in this, my native land. Of course
we all have the privilege of worshipping under our vine
and fig tree, or all except myself, for I suppose I have been
crazy too long to worship any where or any thing; but it
was through Thomas Paine's influence that we now have that
privilege. The most of people swallow what the ministers say about Thomas Paine. The lady that I spoke of
has mouldered back to mother earth long ago. I know
she had superior qualities of mind, but she had some weak
points.

I have a small affair that I wish to bring before the
world, which is an act of injustice done by Mr. Dugger,
an Express Agent in Virden, Ill. In eighteen hundred
and fifty eight I was through the southern part of Illinois
selling books, and when I was at Virden I expressed money
to pay for one thousand books, and I gave it to the agent
in gold. At that time I was afraid to keep bills or even
take one, and I did not know anything about Western
bills, and I had taken particular pains to get it into gold, and
I paid him seventy-five cents for sending it. I received a
box of books while there, and I paid him twelve dollars
on them. I had never expressed money before, but supposed if I handed it to him and took a receipt for it, I was
perfectly safe. When the money got to Syracuse it was
all in Western bills, except five dollars, and that was not
worth one cent nor had not been for months, and there
was a discount on the Western bills, and I knew it. And

when I heard from the printer I found out what they had done, and I wrote to the printer that I had got a receipt for gold. They wrote back and forth, and Mr. Dugger wrote to the printer that I had sold the gold to them for a premium. But I have always heard that it takes two to make a bargain, but certainly that bargain was made without my knowledge or consent, for the word premium was not mentioned to me nor in my presence while I was in the store. They kept a dry goods store; and I did not stop there three moments. It was a young man that received the money, and the same one gave me a receipt, and I have it now. It appears that they did not expect to hear from the case, for they wrote in one of their letters that they did not know whether they gave a receipt for gold or not. I presume that when they took the money they did not think of the plan of speculating on it. But they had sixty-three dollars, and they were not doing much business except attending protracted meetings, and perhaps they made enough on that gold to allow them to contribute liberally to the minister, but they should have been more careful how they made out their receipt. When they found they were caught they made some bold threats to the printer, and I believe said that they had a witness or two to the money bargain. But of course a man who would be guilty of an act of that kind with a lady who was making an honest living for herself, would be guilty of any or every base act that he could make money out of and live in idleness himself. I told the express agent in Chicago that it took a great many witnesses to make one falsehood into a fact. He told me he would settle it with me if he knew that the money was not changed in Syracuse. I can show him the letters that Mr. Dugger wrote to the printer, acknowedging that they sent bills, and I hope they will please to regulate it. The letters read as follows:

{ OFFICE OF THE U. S. EXPRESS Co.
{ LA SALLE, March 12th, 1858.

J. G. K. TRUAIR, Esq.,

DEAR SIR :—In relation to the trick played upon Miss Davis by the Agent at Virden, (mentioned in your letter

to Miss Davis, of March 1st,) I would say that the matter was left with me, by Miss Davis, this day, and has been duly reported by me to the Superintendent, for adjustment.   Yours truly,
J. A. RAYNOR.

{ Office of the U. S. Express Co.
  Virden, March 16th, 1858.

Mr. J. G. K. Truair, Syracuse, N. Y.—

I received through our Superintendent, Mr. Johnson, a note from you, through Miss P. B. Davis, in regard to some exchange on $50 in currency sent to you instead of $50 in gold, as you claim.

Now Miss Davis came into the office with $50 in gold, to be sent to you, but whilst I was making out a receipt for Miss Davis, she sold the gold to Messrs. Dugger & Hagler at a premium of three per cent. The money was delivered to them and currency inserted in the stead. But as to the $5 R. I. Central Bank being put in, I know not, but they have redeemed it. But I would say that if you want to publish it do so, and put in something about a leather strap that was stolen off her trunks, that she made such a fuss about. It is very good that she was not a man or she would got a drubbing or me one.

But mind you, that if you publish anything but the truth, I'll put you through. I have sent through Mr. Johnson, our Superintendent, the deposition of Mr. G. W. Dugger, and have two more that I can send if necessary.
Yours respectfully,
JOHN A. DUGGER, Agent.

{ Office of the U. S. Eppress Co.
  La Salle, March 18th, 1858.

J. G. K. Truair, Esq.,

Dear Sir :—I wrote you a few days since, in relation to Miss Davis and her trouble with our Agent, at Virden. The matter has been duly investigated, by which it appeared Miss Davis went to said Agent with $50 in gold, and gave it to him loose and unpacked, in her open hand, (which is contrary to rules.) The father of the Agent was present, bought the gold of Miss Davis, and paid her the premium, by which she appeared perfectly satisfied.

The $5 R. I. Central money, returned by you to Miss Davis, has been exchanged and a good $5 returned to her in its place. Yours truly,
J. A. RAYNOR.

{ DAILY JOURNAL OFFICE,
SYRACUSE, March 18, 1858.

JOHN A. DUGGER, Agent Express Co., Virden, Illinois,

DEAR SIR:—Yours of the 16th came to hand this morning.

I have only to say that if you gave Miss Davis a receipt for gold you are bound to send gold, and the loss by discount on the $45 is due to me.

I certainly wonder that you should, as an express agent, give a receipt for gold, and send Western bills which you must have known were chargeable in this State with a ruinous discount.

Your threat at the close of your letter is unworthy of you and your office, and will not deter me a moment from exposing, if necessary, what I cannot regard as any other than a dastardly trick imposed upon a woman.

I have confidence in the Superintendent of the Company, and, if necessary, shall transmit your uncourteous letter to him.

All I have asked has been the exchange of the Rhode Island bill, and the payment of the $4\frac{1}{2}$ per cent. discount.
Yours, &c., J. G. K. TRUAIR.

VIRDEN, Ill., March 23, 1858.

J. G. K. TRUAIR, Syracuse. N. Y.:

Yours of the 18th is at hand. In reply, as to the receipt for gold I cannot say, perhaps may be, do not recollect.

It is generally the habit for persons who transmit money by express, to do up their own packages. In this case

Miss Davis did not; she gave or laid it on the desk from her open hands. I wrote a receipt for the same, and was called by some one, and did not pack it up at that moment, but when I got through and came back, Messrs. Dugger & Hagler purchased the gold from her at three per cent. premium.

As to the R. I. Bank, I know nothing about it; but I gave Mr. Johnson, (our Superintendent,) another in its stead.

There were two persons who were present when the transaction occurred, and can say the same.

Truly yours, JOHN A. DUGGER.

I told the Agent in Chicago that I should publish it, and that he did not wish me to do. I told him I would publish them all, just as I found them. I found that they had an idea of being rather independent in the office at Chicago, and I told them I did not fear the lower classes; I saw their motive at once, which was to frighten me out of it.

McArthur was the Agent in Burlington, Iowa, and I expressed money there, and took a witness along with me; I told him what it was for, and I thought he was a young Mount Etna for a few moments. He told me that Mr. Dugger had two or three men that would take oath to the premium bargain. I saw their sympathies were with the dishonest, and by what I have seen since I have been in the business, I am obliged to believe that an honest man is rather a scarce article in this world. I have frequently thought that men had more native honor than women, but experience has told me better.

While I was at Virden I left my trunks at the depot, and when I went after them I found they had taken a leather strap from one of them. I know it was not worth but twenty-five cents here, but there I had to pay fifty cents for one, and I thought I had a right to tell them of it at the depot, which I did, and asked them to pay me for it or get me another. Mr. Dugger mentioned the strap in his letter, and I was glad he did, for I had forgotten that; but I hope I shall get the whole together after a while. If I had gone into Virden and went to stealing trifles from

Mr. Dugger, or the Agent at the depot, I am thinking I should have heard from them. I only ask the same that they would under the same circumstances, but I should find myself in jail for taking twenty-five cents. They have advertised me rather loud, as the woman said, on the telegraph wires, and their advertisements are rather derogatory to character, where one is not known.

When I go to Buffalo I shall see the general Express Agent, and I am told that he is a straight-forward man, and he will see my receipt and their impudent threats to the printer, which, if a man was innocent, he would never make.

## CHAPTER VI.

As I have traveled rather extensively through a number of the different States in the Union, I will give a brief sketch of the prominent traits of character of the people in each State. Massachusetts being the oldest State, of course her public institutions are first in the United States. Their facilities for education have always been superior to the rest so far. The most of our great scholars originate from Boston and its vicinity, and all progression, or nearly all, both moral and intellectual, have their foundation in that old puritanic city. They have a high tone of moral feeling, and you will find a high moral head and a long physiognomy, and very prominent intellect, and great perceptive faculties, and rather social, but dignified. Their heads are very smooth and well developed. It is not so much the quantity of brain as it is the quality that furnishes great powers of mind, and their brain rather predominates over the physical system, and many of them are victims for consumption, for their lungs will not support their brain. When I traveled through there I found that they were narrow in their feelings and views, compared with the Western people. They hold on to the half penny deal yet, but I find that when they emigrate West and settle there, their views and feelings become enlarged, and they are apt to drop the sulphur out of their religion, and as a Western gentlemen told me, "the Yankees carried a great many vices out West, and the choicest of virtues." I told him that foreigners had flocked into America until they had robbed the working classes of a living, for a Yankee would not work for nothing, and the Irish were so numerous that their help could be got for much less than the Yankee would work for. Before the Western world opened up resources for the Eastern people, there was a class of young men who had become, or had grown up very reckless, for they felt that they had been robbed of their rights by foreign paupers, and so they have. There is no nation of people that I have ever seen who would work by the side of the railroad Irish. Not even the slaves in the South are willing to work side by side with the Irish, and they would kill one for two words of impudence.

The bandits who infest the Western world are stray individuals from all over creation, as they say there, but reading their history I found that many of them were of Eastern origin, and that some of the greatest intellects in the world were engaged in the blackest of crimes. One out of three, while on the gallows, spoke two hours, and he said that there was nearly three hundred in the company that he belonged to, and they had robbed a great many, but they never had much money on hand at once, because they always assisted all the poor that they ever met, and he said that they never meant to take life. Their noble traits go to show that they were misguided minds, and their moral feelings were perverted, for their object was not to kill or to hoard up, but they were victims of circumstances; but the wheat and the tares grow on the same soil.

The Massachusetts people are a class who want a great deal, and are rather inclined to be miserly, but they are very industrious, and always want a large house to live in. Even the poor classes will invest every cent they have in a great shell of a house, whether they need it or not, or ever can furnish it. They appear to think that an empty mansion is the beginning of wisdom; I did not know that until I had traveled through the State. But I found them very kind and clean. They have large order and ideality, and they are apt to be rather tall, and they have more mental aristocracy than New York has because they have more intelligence. Boston affords two kinds of aristocracy, the literary and the fashionable, while the Western States only afford the fashionable class. But even the literary class in Boston liberalize their feelings very much by traveling through the Western States. The old Puritans are very narrow in their religious views, for their brain has not scope enough. The mass of the people through the Eastern States are harmoniously small as long

as they stay there, for the circumstances that surround
them are small in some respects; but I could not see these
things while I lived there myself, and they do not see them
until they leave there.

My ancestry are all natives of Massachusetts. My
father was born on what was once called Cape Ann, in the
town of Gloucester, south of Boston, and my father's moth
er taught school for a living when she was a young lady.
Grand-father moved into Vermont in rather an early day,
when he had to carry his grain thirty miles to the mill.
and on his shoulders at that, and stay all night to get his
grist and return the next day. Vermont was settled by
emigrants from Massachusetts, and many of them were
very intelligent men, though some of them were not as
intelligent as others. Vermont is rather more of an inland
State than any other of the New England States, for there
is no seaport town in the State, and there has been less to
contaminate the morals of the people in Vermont than any
other State in the Union, until quite recently. The railroads have invited more of the variety into the State than
there has ever been there before, and they now lock their
doors at night; but in the town where I was brought up,
as long as I lived there, I never saw a lock on an outside
door in my life, and we generally left every outside door
open during the warm weather. One of our old merchants
often went to Boston after goods, and he had traveled
more than any other man in town, and he always said that
Vermont had the most moral class of women of any State
that he had ever been in.

When I was in Mississippi a getnleman told me of a
school teacher from Vermont. He said that a Southerner
got provoked at him for a very trivial circumstance, and
killed him in a moment with a dirk knife. He said that
the young man was as much of a stranger to fighting as a
child three years of age. I told him that nearly all of
them were twenty-five years ago; but now I think it is the
most moral State in the Union. But they are small in
their deal until they emigrate, and then they enlarge their
views, and are very enterprising. In the Western States
they are called the most intellectual class that emigrate

from New England. They say that New York furnishes the most in number, and they are very sharp, shrewd, and enterprising, but the most of them are descendants from the different Yankee States. The English say that the Yankees are a shrewd and calculating class of people, that they will live where they would starve. I think they are all very similar in their characters. The Connecticut people are rather mechanical, ingenious, and intellectual. As far as I went into the State I liked them very well, and I like them wherever I find them. The Yankees have what I call tact, that gives them the ability to apply their talent in a way that no other class of people that I have seen are possessed of; and the low and vulgar have no other name for Yankee tact than insanity. Everything that a Yankee does or says that the thick skulls cannot understand, they call insanity or infidelity.

But I was through Canada West, and the English there have very comprehensive minds, their heads are very broad, and they are self-possessed and dignified. I seldom saw one that was excitable, and they understand the Yankee very quick, for their eye is on us, and they know very well that we are a branch of the English nation, and they would be proud of us if we were not so trickish. But the Yankees and English get along very well together in Canada, for there is a very fine class of English there, and I felt very much at home with them. You will find the solids in their character, and in their government they are not to be bought and sold for trifles. An English gentleman is a gentleman at home and abroad, and if he is your friend you have a friend. Both the Yankee and the English are benefitted by living together, the English wear the half-penny deal out of the Yankee, and the Yankee imparts his off hand way of doing business to the English, and therefore they derive a mutual benefit by associating together. The old prejudice is wearing away, the more they know each other they better they think of each other. They mean to be very judicious, and they are rather generous, and appreciate merit and character, and every nice quality of mind. They have liberal views, and whenever they change their government it is always for the better, and the Queen is a great and good specimen of the great brotherhood of mankind; she is an extra chip from the block of nature, and a true woman and a perfect lady, and every way worthy of her position, because she is qualified to do justice in all cases and in all places, and under all circumstances. She has liberated a great many American criminals who were banished for high treason, and I wish she would come to America and give our ladies some lessons on just principles and generous feelings. On the whole I admire the English character, and I found a great many congenial spirits in Canada. The English all say that they can tell a Yankee by their walk, they are more elastic in their constitutions than any other people, and rather sapre, and thin favored, and as the English say; they will not plod, and if there is a good place the Yankee will find it.

I found some Scotch in my travels, and I thought very much of them generally, especially those who are educated. I seldom found a Scotchman living in a large house, and I hardly ever found one without money or good books, such as histories. They understand character very well, and they have a just appreciation of merit, motives and enterprise, and they are very industrious. When I was selling even my small pamphlet the Scotch not only thought it was a laudable enterprise, but they appreciated the writing of a book as an accomplishment, and the most bought books of me.

But neither the Scotch nor English think as much of dress as the Yankees do, but they are very good capitalists. I think it is the Highland Scotch that are the best educated. When the educated Scotch come to America they look for high positions, they want an office. They have plenty of self esteem, and are rather apt to be tyranical until they have been here a long time; but they generally feel qualified to govern the world. But I found them to be a very knowing people, and a people of good native character. The Scotch ladies are apt to be readers as well as the gentlemen, and they generally have very good scholarship and a high tone of feeling.

The few French that I saw I liked very well, or the class

that were educated. The French Catholics that I saw in Canada were illiterate, and hardly looked like human beings, but all the French that I have ever met who were brought up in France, I have found to be very pleasant people. There is a very good class in Montreal, I suppose much better than in Quebec. As a people, they are very quick and polite, and very refined in their tastes. Their brain is very easily disturbed, for they are very sensitive, and there is more insanity in France than in any other nation in the world. The Americans are the second in that respect, especially the New Englanders and their descendants.

I think we had less Dutch patients in the Institution during the time that I was there than any other nation, according to the number that there are in America. Yet I am certain of the fact that I know that there was one man and his wife there at the same time, as patients; but she had a very fine temperament for a Dutch lady. In selling my books it was not often that I came across a Dutch person who was nervous, for they generally have a phlegmatic temperament. They are organized for plodding, and they do plod. While the Yankee is tearing his brain all to pieces to reach something new, the Dutchman is moving along as though there was nothing more to be known, and they enjoy life; but as a people they are not the ready beings that the French are.

I was in Pennsylvania, and found that the first German settlers had neglected to educate their children. They thought more of money and land than they did of education, and not until a few years past have they ever had free schools established, and I saw a great many young people who could not read one word, and very good disposed people, too. They are now beginning to see their weak points, and they are a very industrious and enterprising people, and quite mechanical, and if their powers of mind were developed they would be very intellectual. But they have not the refined tastes that the Yankees have, and they are not generally as clean as the Yankees are. They are naturally very honorable, and they are disposed to respect the New England people, for they send there for a great many school teachers. They appear to know that knowledge is power, and I found that wherever the Yankee has been, or wherever he goes, he makes his impressions. He is not led, but he leads the van, and he makes everything tell that he takes hold of. I found it was the general opinion of all classes and nations that the precocious Yankee was the effect of free schools that were established in New England in an early day, when the first generation were children. And now that old Puritan class transmit the first quality of brains to their children, and they are destined to be the greatest people in the world; but they had ought to marry and intermarry with the English and Dutch.

I was through the Western States, and I found that the Western people were very fond of the Yankees, when they became acquainted with them. They employ them as teachers, and like them for teachers, for a number told me that the children would learn more of an Eastern teacher in three months than they would of a Western teacher in three years. But that class were descendants of the Pennsylvania Dutch, and very many of the Ohio people regret very much that their ancestry neglected to educate their children; but they are now making an effort to improve themselves and educate their children.

The Western reserve is mostly settled by Connecticut Yankees, and their influence is felt all through the State. The Anglo Saxon blood does more to develope the resources of a country than all the rest of creation; the expression of their countenances denotes that, for they are born with that anxious, ready look, that speaks for itself, and tells the world that they have a mark to make before they leave it. The English give weight where the Yankees make a point. The English have the greatest navy of any nation in the world, and the French have the most soldiers.

I was through Michigan, and found the people very friendly indeed, and felt very much at home there. But I found a great many Eastern people there, and the northern part of Illinois is alive with Yankees, and some of all classes. The rich prairie land is what they are after, and they have got it, too; but the best locations are taken up, yet, during tne financial crisis, land was much lower than it has been for a number of years past. I found the people very liberal there, and all glad to see a Yankee. It is very warm there in the summer and very cold in the winter, for there is no forest land in many parts of Illinois and Iowa to break the wind that often sweeps everything before it, on the level prairie; most of them build their houses rather low on that account. They cannot raise fruit there, for what snow they have, the wind gathers up in a hurry and distributes it in every direction, leaving the roots of the trees unprotected in the winter, and they die out, but on some of the rolling land they have very good fruit. The soil is from two to seven feet deep, and it rests on a bed of clay; it cannot leach much, and will bear drouth very well. Some suppose that all the prairie land has once been timbered over, for they say in ploughing deep they often plough up roots of old trees, and they think it took fire by electricity, and the prairie grass was so stubborn that it destroyed all the timber. They say that it has been burned over a great many times, and there is now a law to prohibit its being set on fire. There have been some whole families burned to death by it in an early day, and they have sometimes suppressed it by ditching; but it is a sublime sight to see what they call a small fire on the Western prairie. They say the prairie grass or the atmosphere, or both, will cure the heaves in horses, and all cases of consumptive people, if they will only go there in time; some think it is the oxygen in the atmosphere, but I was told of great cures out there.

I did not see much difference in the habits and customs of the natives of Illinois, Iowa and Indiana, they were all kind to me. Some think that they are rather jealous of the Eastern people, but I think it is wearing out, on the strength of a better knowledge of them in the southern part of Illinois.

I found a great many emigrants from the different Southern States, and they were the most generous class of people that I ever saw in my life. Emigration has the tendency to liberalize and subdue, the Americans in particular, and to develope the mind, and if a person has a

mind as large as a peanut it will call it out. I never saw
but one Southerner in a free State who was small in his
deal, and he was not very poor, and they were not poor
enough to be small. They were very fond of the Yankees,
for the most of the Yankees treat them with civility.

I was as far as St. Paul and St. Anthony, in Minesota,
and there was any number of Yankees among the variety
of classes. I was in Peoria, Ill., and there was the mixed
multitude, and I sold books to all classes except the Catholic Irish. But the Irish from the northern part of Ireland
are Protestants, and some of them are very intelligent, and
do their own thinking. Once in a great while I sold a
copy to a Catholic, but in some cases I found it was dangerous to go within their reach after they had read it, because I told the truth about their treatment to the patients
in the Lunatic Asylum. The Irish have no right there as
attendants, and the low Irish have no right there as patients,
for I think it one of the greatest of crimes for Americans
to be compelled to associate with those low cattle of Irish
under any circumstances whatever, not even in a criminal
institution, much less a benevolent institution, for what
lady would think of choosing one of the old flat-faced,
brawling Irish women who are seen going to church and
muttering along and counting their beads, for a companion
or an associate. Yet we had that very class in the Asylum with the most intellectual class in the house; and the
American attendants all spoke of it, for their influence, or
feelings and habits were enough to disgust the swine.
There was one old stump there who would groan out " be
Jasus," from morning until night, and I often told her that
I thought that Jesus was very sorry that he happened to
have that name, and if she would coin some other word or
name it would be quite a change to the patients, but the
next breath would be a groan, and " be Jasus" on the end
of it. Her groans were to my ears more like the drawing
of a stone-boat over a macadamized street than they were
like a sound made by one of Adam's race; but, however,
" be Jasus" was along every time. She was better acquainted with his name than she was with his character.

I have not thought of the Quakers, although I am not

n.. :h acquainted with them as a people. What I have seen of them they are distant and forbidding, very austere, and remarkably selfish and penurious. Wherever they go they establish order and ideality, and their religion is made up of those two organs. They remind me of the old man's prayer, when he prayed for himself and his wife, his son John and his wife, they four and no more. But the Quakers are very clean and industrious, and the most of them are wealthy, for they do not spend all for dress and fashion. They never have poor houses, and they always take care of their own poor, and that is a redeeming trait of character, it is humane, and all christians should do it, for that certainly is a vein of christianity. Occasionally they bought a book of me, and they were extremely inquisitive. They always educate their children, for they are very intelligent and quiet, and if one is generous they are generous indeed. But I made up my mind that question asking did got belong to the Yankees.

The New Jersey people that I saw were certainly the meanest class of beings that can live, except the lowest class of Irish; they were very illiterate and very ugly.

## CHAPTER VII.

I will now attempt to give a ragged description of my observations and experience during the time that I spent in the Southern States, which was nearly a year. I was not in Florida, nor Texas, nor Arkansas, but I passed through the others, and spent some time in the most of them. My business was such that it gave me an opportunity of becoming acquainted with the social condition of all classes and colors, and shades of the same color, both rich and poor and bond and free. I did not fail to observe correctly, for I will not allow myself to be blinded by prejudice, neither will I exaggerate to swell small streams into broad seas, for the sake of making money at the expense of the feelings or character of individuals or a people in general. I wish to be just, not only to myself, but to the world, and I am well aware that a candid person had much rather read a book made up of facts that they can rely upon, than a work that is thrown together simply to feed up popular opinion, such as sacrifice principle to popularity. I do not claim to be a fashionable nor a rational authoress, for the matter of fact principle was established in my nature long before I left the farmer's kitchen. I was thrown upon my own resources, in high life, where the lady of the house was not at home if she happened to be engaged in her domestic affairs, as she ought to be a portion of her time. I find that it is rather hard for me to dispose of the crazy habit of telling the trutn, if I tell anything at all, and the merit of my writing is based on the truth of what I write, for my style of writing is more like a Virginia fence than it is like well arranged composition, written in good language ; but perhaps my motives are as good as those who can write smooth, and, as the Dutch say, use great big words. I did try to select a few of the best words for my other pamphlet, and I rather overdone the business and got one great word that many people could not pronounce, and I thought proper to leave that out or divide it into three or four short ones, and find room for them somewhere. I hope community will please to bear with my weak points, and take the will for the deed, and read my opinion on the institution of slavery, which will not be in accordance with all opinions, that are entirely ignorant of the true social condition of the slaves, and also of the white people.

I found the majority of the white people to be very illitterate, for free schools have been considered an anomaly in all the Southern States until quite recently, and now a slaveholder that cannot read nor write his own name thinks it a disgrace to send his children to a free school, for the simple reason that they must mingle with the poor white children, and perhaps the man himself had been as poor as a man could be. But many fine specimens of the human family in the South had not means to send their children to select schools there, for they are like angels' visits, few and far between, until within a few years. I think the rail roads are doing very much to settle up the country, and I hope to civilize the white people, for in nearly all the small villages on all the railroads that I traveled over I found that they had a school house, and in some of the small villages they had two, a free school and a select school. The very poor white people were living in the most abject poverty of any class of human beings that I ever saw in my life. Their principle food was what they call hog and hominy, and coffee without either sugar or milk. Their hog, as they call it, is certainly the poorest pork that I ever saw in my life; I tried to eat it a few times but I could not, and I was obliged to finish my meal on pone, which is their name for one way of cooking corn meal. It is made up of cold water and Indian meal, and when baked is as hard as cemented gravel, and about as coarse as gravel, and relished about as well as gravel cake would baked in the ashes. Their pork was all smoked, and the most of it covered with yellow rust, and even the gravy with that pone was equal to medicine. But they do not aspire above their present condition. They were not a clean people by any means, neither were they filthy like the low class of foreigners that come to America. I saw a great many of that very poor class, and when I told them I was selling books perhaps their reply would be, "What mout your name be?" and after telling my name the next question would be, "did you fotch these books all the way here alone by yourself?" and then, "I s'pose you Yankees dont dip snuff, du ye?" I told them we did not, and then they take their stick, that they chew up until it becomes a swab or a young mop, as I often told them, and dive it into the snuff and rub their teeth and mouth, and then keep the snuff end in one side of their mouth and the clean end out apiece, looking as though they were going to build a fire. The most of them are very dirty about their snuff, except it be the higher classes, and some of them were, although they did not all use it, but the most of them do. The fashionable class are shy about it, and there are some now that begin to think it a vulgar habit. I have seen children five years of age dipping snuff, and boys three and four years of age chewing tobacco, and gentlemen almost make food of it, and one would know that to go into their business establishments or offices, for the walls and floors are finished with fresco work, or the most of them, there a few who have a great deal of order, both ladies and gentlemen. The most of the Southerners are very deficient in the organ of order, but they all have got great powers of discrimination. Even the lower classes know the well bred, and if they are not vicious they treat strangers with great respect. But the railroads have called a class out of the mountains who live as I have described, and a great many of them are very needy indeed. A person might trade there a long time, and unless their business was similar to my own, they would not be likely to see the variety of classes that I did, and would hardly know that there were such people as I have described, but they are all there, and more too.

The slaves feel themselves far superior to the poor white people. They are rather encouraged in the idea that if a white man does not own slaves he is the most despiseable being on earth, not even fit for them to associate with; but I think it is **decidedly wrong in the slave-**

holder to do that. The slaveholder does not treat the poor white man with any more respect than he does his slaves, and if he wants to hire help he will hire another man's slaves in preference to giving work to the poor white man, he has no chance for his life. The poor live in log houses and very light framed houses, and one-half of them will not have a window in them, but perhaps they will have tight outside blinds, and when it is rather cool they are obliged to close them and leave the door open, and see to work by the light that comes down chimney, and they have to sit close to the fire place to dispose of their snuff saliva. A cooking stove is a stranger to thousands of people in the South, but they are beginning to use them in some places. They are rather awkward with all kinds of stoves, for they do not have occasion to keep them red hot for six months in the year, as we do here. But as they clear up the land the cold weather grows more severe, and the wind reaches them more than it formerly has, and it is summer there in the morning and winter in the afternoon. They are subject to sudden changes quite far South, and more or less so in the most of the Southern States until they strike Texas and Florida. And why they are in some parts more than others, is because the bleak winds from the Rocky mountains sweep over certain portions of the South. When one of those tornadoes start out it is heard for a long distance, and will come tearing and roaring through the tall yellow pine groves as though it had brought the greatest storm along with it that ever was known. The force of it is very much broken by the forest before it reaches cleared land, but if it did not lose its force before it reached dwellings it would make hard work. When that wind strikes one they feel it, and talk of a right smart wind; but they pass over and no rain is seen. They said that it was very dangerous to be in one of those pine forests during the wind and weather, for the pine timber is very tall, and being full of turpentine the limbs are as heavy as lead, and if a limb falls on one it is very apt to be felt, as most of the limbs are very near the top of the trees. It is the most beautiful timber that I ever saw in my life, but the carpenters told me that it was very hard to work, and would never wear out, for it is impervious to wind and weather. It is quick wood, and the smoke is very similar to the the bituminous coal smoke, and thousands of poor folks never have a candle in their houses, but they have a fire light made of that pine, and they eat supper by the light of a pine torch stuck into a crack in the wall of the house. I have eat with them in that way, and even by fire light without a torch or candle I was posted on the variety of food, which was hog and hominy, and I have paid one dollar per day for board, and perhaps three beds in one room, and two or three in each bed. One night I slept with a woman and three children, as it would have cost me two dollars per day for board. In that house there were three grown persons, and one out of the three could just make out to read the title-page to my book by spelling out the words, and some of the slaves can do as much as that. Some of the white children will teach the slave children how to read, which does not show total depravity in the children as much as it does in the slaveholders who make laws to prohibit the slaves being sent to school. It is against the law in some of the Southern States, and I do not know but all of them, to educate the slaves, some of the free Africans can read, and in a clandestine way they often teach the shrewd slaves, but they had better not be caught at it.

The slaveholder is planting thorns that will spring up and prick him, for many of the mulattoes are much more shrewd than their half-brothers and sisters that are white. Eventually the mixed blood will emancipate the whole, for the old ones will die off, and it is very seldom I saw a family of young slaves with more than one or two or three of the pure Africans among them, and I very often saw children, and some young men and women, that I thought were white until I got close to them. I often asked them questions when I was out selling books, to sound their minds, the children in particular, both black and white, and the mulattoes were ten per cent. the brightest of the whole South, except that they were robbed of their education. Some of them have the first quality of English blood in them, and it is rather hard to whip that out of them. And they have found that out, and they treat the first-class mulattoes very different from the more ordinary class of slaves. They generally make house servants of the delicate mulattoes, such as they belong in their own families, the half-brothers and sisters as I call them, for they very often resemble each other very much. They often dress that class very well, and their work does not require the strong clothing that the field slaves wear. When the white children marry off and leave home the mulatto brothers and sisters are generally given to them for house servants. I have sometimes found them to know much more than their masters and mistresses, for their white fathers were obliged to transact business on a large scale, which developes their brain on a large scale. The business class of Southerners have very large heads and a full brain, and the mother of the half white children works, and although her brain is not generally well balanced, yet many of them have full brains, not favorable to good morals, but just as good as she can be while robbed of every natural right by the master, who is no better than herself, and at the same time is capable of knowing more and being better.

The slaveholder works hard to take care of his slaves, and the slaves work to take care of their masters, but the white women are so illiterate that they imagine themselves on a level with the slaves if they do anything for themselves or the world, and we cannot expect a very intellectual class of ladies out of that condition of things. But I think that within a few years the Southern ladies are rather more industrious than they formerly have been, for I found that they all appreciated the industrious habits of the Northern people. All of them acknowledged that the Northern people were in advance of the South in every respect except anti-slavery, and that in the South it is the bane of their lives, and many of them see the wrongs because they look at the results. They measure the future by what they observe of the laws of nature, for they find that the Africans are not the fools that they once were. I suppose the anti-slavery party have done very much to soften down their government to their slaves, in some respects.

I was told some facts in confidence by a Southern lady, and she was a true lady to every one. They, said she, did not care how soon the slaves were emancipated, if they could all take care of themselves, but she said they were not qualified for that now, neither could they be at present, for they are treated like children, and have no business talent developed, and if thrown upon their own resources they would not know where to begin life as well as a family of young children. Until they are men grown, and even until they are thirty and forty years of age they call them boys, and when they get quite old they call them uncle and aunt, which sounds very pleasant and respectful.

The most of the white women know so little that they cannot do much to mould the minds of the young slaves, for they are hardly capable of transmitting common sense to their own children, and as long as the white people are so ignorant there, and the slaves much more so, it does not seem hardly proper to dispose of slavery by direct emancipation at present, for the slaveholder has brutalized the Africans to keep them in slavery until they have lost the manly nature that they would have had if they had been treated as they should have been. They very well know that they cannot enslave an intelligent mind, and to make a bright child a willing slave they have got to take particular pains to do it. Every one in the house will speak to him as though he were a dog, for they know how to blunt all of his sensibilities. Even young white children know how to treat the slaves, and an old slave must obey a white child five years of age. The slaves will often say that their skin is black, but their blood is as red as a white person's. I found that they were not all willing slaves, but once in a while I saw a child who was made a great pet of by the white people, but after all he must grow up as servile as the lowest African that lives, or they say he will get above his business, and perhaps run away. If he happens to have an intelligent master, and his master finds out that he is honest, he always treats him well, for he always makes more of a good slave than he can of a dishonest one, for on a large plantation it is very convenient to have slaves that can be trusted, for one man cannot transact all the business on a plantation, and it is only the very few who can be trusted. If a man can trust his slaves it saves him the expense of hiring a white man.

I like liberty and freedom, and it belongs to the constitution of the United States, but there is reason in all things, and I think it is a great question to know how to dispose of slavery, for I should fear the consequences if done in haste. I have talked with some very candid Southern gentlemen about it, and they said that if it was an evil it would wear itself out, and that candid class of men thought it was an evil, and that it would be a very dangerous evil to free them all at once. I told them that I thought if the Northern people would go in there and educate the white people and the slaveholders, and civilize them, and prepare them to know what civilization is, they would learn after a while now to treat the Africans, for we know now that they do not know how to treat each other, and it is not to be expected that they will know how to treat the Africans when three quarters of the inhabitants of the South are barbarians.

The Southerners say that the Northerners do not understand the social condition of the slaves, if they did they think there would be no trouble between the North and the South, and I am inclined to think that would be the case myself. I think they would treat the subject very different, and without any hard feelings between the North and the South. I met Northern people there who had been very rabid abolitionists, and I took particular pains to get their opinions, and I found that they had changed in their feelings and opinions very much. When they come to see three or four millions of slaves, and see that the base of their brain predominates, and how many less white people there are than slaves, they then begin to reflect upon the wrong steps that the anti-slavery party have taken, for no one can know what the African race are collectively until they go South and spend some time, and see them in all conditions, and see how undeveloped they are. Yet I pity their helpless condition, especially those who are capable of being men and women, but I should pity them more **to see them all emancipated to-day than I did to see them** as I did the most of them. As near as I could judge from what I saw, I should think that about one quarter of them were treated very humane, but yet there was the moral slavery connected with the humanity shown to them. But the force of habit is so strong that we cannot impress their minds with our ideas of the subject certainly by brute force, for they have a very high tone of feeling. Their feeling of resentment is very strong, and that class can only be influenced by moral treatment. The slaves that belong to that class of men nearly worship their masters and mistresses, and they are the ones that expose the class of slaves that engage in planning insurrections, for they think just as much of their masters as their own children do. And that class of masters have well disciplined minds themselves, and they are not apt to have colored children in their own families, and they will not strike or whip a grown slave, but they will try to have them do right, and if they cannot control them they will sell them down South, as they call it, which means New Orleans. There they are put on to a very large plantation and subjected to the lash for outbreaks, and when one of that class of slaves are whipped they whip them just as long as they dare to. I was told that they often died very soon after the Southern plantation whippings; but such cases are generally done by the overseers out on the plantation, and there is no one to witness it except the slaves, and their oath is not allowed in any case except against each other. A slave stands a very poor chance of his life out on one of those plantations, two or three miles from any white person except the overseer, and it is no loss to him, and the master often lives quite a distance from his plantation, and a slave might be dead for some time and he not know it, where a man owns five or six hundred, or a thousand field slaves. It is no small job to gather them all in and count them, and if there is one missing the rest of them do not dare to say anything about it. There are a great many cabins on a large plantation, and the slaves are not apt to be in, or not all of them, except at meal time and Sabbath days, and the master is generally at home then himself, and in working hours it would consume too much time to arrange the slaves for counting them correctly.

I was told by the first class of slaveholders that many a slave murder passed for the reasons that I have spoken of. There is a law for the slaves, but the trouble is in reaching all cases on the very large plantations, and the overseers all know that very well. A man that has only a few slaves is more liable to get found out than those who own a great many, for he is very apt to have near neighbours, but that does not prevent all classes of abuses to the slaves. But one is not as apt to get whipped to death directly as they are further off, but they are more apt to get the variety of small every day abuses, than they are on a large plantation. But the slaves on the large plantations are made up of the odds and ends of all the Southern States, and they are just about such a class of criminals as there are in the State Prisons throughout the United States, all the difference is that one class is black and the other is white.

When we talk of freeing all those slaves at the same time, we might with equal propriety talk of letting out all the convicts, and allow them to run at large at their leisure. When I speak of that they all say at once that we should have a state of semi-barbarism. And there is only a handful of prisoners compared with three or four millions of slaves that would be entirely helpless off of a cotton plantation. They have no education, and they cannot do anything else; it would be like turning a large drove of cattle upon a sandy desert.

I can tell the world that among the slaves on the very large plantations there is a concentration of evil in a condensed form, and I think that amalgamation will eventually emancipate the Africans. Slavery and its consequences cover a great piece of ground. The Anglo Saxon blood is finding its way among the Africans at a very rapid rate, and it is not to be whipped out either. The gentlemen and ladies both told me that the mulattoes were much harder to govern than the pure Africans were; they said they were very apt to be impudent. I have seen them appear as independent as their white fathers do, and I think the negress that the white man associates with is just as good

as himself, for he chooses to make her his equal in some
respects, and she has a right to claim to be his equal in all
respects. But the idea of eating with one of their colored
children is almost equal to high treason there. Their ideas
of justice do not harmonize very well, and their tastes are
very dissimilar, but they have been brought up in that
heterogeneous mass of corruption, and to take them out in
their present state of ignorance they would have no motive
to live for. The most of them live to dissipate, and they
do not think anything of taking life among the white peo-
people. For the least offense, for two or three short words,
either a pistol or a dirk is presented, and the murderer is
allowed to go at large, or at least they are not dealt with
very severely, unless it is a premeditated murder for
money, and then they deal differently with them. They
are more severe than they have been, but the slave is either
burned or executed for the same class of crimes that are
rather tolerated in the slaveholder. They consider the
Africans very inferior, and yet they make them legally
responsible for crimes that the white man is privileged
to commit, which is a very inconsistent idea, for how can
they expect a stream of water to rise above the fountain
it springs from. The slaves have their masters' example
there the same as a family have the example of their parents here; their masters murder each other, and the
slaves murder their masters, but I do not think there is as
many white men murdered by the slaves as there is slaves
murdered by the white men. What would the slaveholder
do or say if he should have the good luck to get to Abra-
ham's bosom, and find some of his slaves there with their
backs completely lashed to rags, I am thinking he would
call on the rocks and the mountains to fall on them instead
of having cowhides to drive them out, as they do at the
South.

I once asked an old slave on a steamboat if her master
was kind to her, and she said that they were all good when
asleep. I thought of my own case, that my friends were
all good when aslsep. But, nevertheless, I am obliged to
think that the true home for the African is in the Southern
States, for there is where they first originated, and the soil

and climate seem to be adapted to their natures. The true Africans are physically organized for plodding, they are coarse built, and have low moral natures, broad shoulders, strong lungs, slow temperaments, and every way built for strength and long life. I hardly ever saw a slave that was what we call round shouldered, or bent forward; they are more likely to bend back than they are to stoop, but occasionally I saw an aged one who looked as though they had always seen hard times. They are not built for consumption, neither are the white people South as much as the Northern people are, the Yankees in particular, yet the consumption is slowly finding its way into the Southern States; it is generally the white people that die with it, but I heard of a few cases among some of the slaves. The slaves have the best teeth, the whitest and the handsomest of any class of people that I ever saw in my life. I was told by a number of ladies that there was never a slave known who could not sing, and I have heard some of them play the violin and other musical instruments very beautifully. They enjoy and have many privileges that we do not know of until we go there. It is quite often that their masters give them a bit of land to raise what they can, and sell the produce for their own benefit, or give them a load of wood to sell for themselves, and the slave is found, and has his master's team to use, and the money is his own, and that they do just as they choose with. Some of them carried splendid gold watches and wore other jewelry, with clothes to correspond, and, indeed, many of the house slaves dressed quite tasty.

I suppose a moral negress in the South is what the atmosphere is not prolific of, and they are all good alike and bad alike, for there is no restraint because immorality is no disgrace to the negress. Those who can wear the most finery feel themselves of great importance in the world. One white person in the Northern States will accomplish quite as much as three slaves will the year round. The slaves say that to work quick is not the way to last, and their masters and mistresses are not exacting of them at all. They do not expect as much of them as people do of **hired help, and it is to their interest to be kind to the** slaves, where they have not many, for if they want to sell one he will sell for more if he is well, or sound, as they say, than one that is broken down or has his back all cut to pieces with a rawhide, unless he is wanted for a large plantation, and then if he is well, his ugly traits are not objectionable. When they are sick they have the best medical attendance that the country affords, and they are not hurried out to work until they are well.

Some Northern people think it is hard to have the food measured out to them, but if the master did not do it they would steal and waste a fortune in one month, but if they have enough it makes no difference, and then there is a law to regulate that; a slaveholder cannot allow his slaves to go hungry if it is known. In Maryland if the master does not keep his slaves comfortable, they can all go to the jail and give themselves up to be sold. The jailor locks them up and advertises them for sale, and the master only gets what he can for them under such circumstances.

## CHAPTER VIII.

"THE TYRANTS OF THE HOUSEHOLD.—And so it is, and for his rule over his family, and for his conduct to wife and children—subjects over whom his power is monarchical, any one who watches the world must look with trembling, sometimes, of the account which many a man will have to render. For in our society there is no law to control the King of the Fireside. He is master of property, happiness, life, almost. He is free to punish, to make happy or unhappy, to ruin or to torture. He may kill a wife gradually, and be no more questioned than the grand seignor who drowns a slave at midnight. He may make slaves and hypocrites of his children; or friends and freemen; or drive them into revolt and enmity against the natural law of love. I have heard politicians and coffee-house wiseacres over the newspaper, railing at the tyranny of the French King, and the Emperor, and wonder how these (who are monarchs, too, in their way,) govern their own dominions at home, where each man rules absolute! When the annals of each little reign are shown to the Supreme Master, under whom we hold sovereignty, histories will be laid bare of household tyrants as cruel as Amurath, and as savage as Nero, and as reckless and dissolute as Charles."

I know that oppression has been the mental battle-axe to suppress intellectual pursuits, but they are just as rabid in the free States in that respect as they are in the South, according to the authority they have. The anti-slavery party are the most tyrannical people there are in the Northern States, and a great many of them make perfect slaves of their wives and children. To be sure a man may not enslave his wife's mind by taking a cowhide and trying to beat her brains out by striking her on her back. But there are a great many strings to pull upon to torture a person that are too intricate to be described by language, and yet it is the most terrible torture to be borne that can be imagined; this is done by the subtle and designing, who generally pass for very amiable people. I found out years ago that the amiable class were the worst class of human beings that I ever knew in my life; I never knew where to find them.

When any of the fashionable vulgar class are in the society of their superiors, it is amusing to see them try to create a low excitement to drown one's voice, because substantial facts are a great annoyance to them.

Slavery will not always exist in the present form, but just as long as one man or woman can find a subject to rule in any part of creation, just so long tyranny will be the hobby. A community will select some individual whom they think is superior, to stab with their tongues, and when they all see that they are about to lose a victim it is very amusing to see them go around from house to house, just like a hungry dog, to look out or up some dirty job to start up an excitement. I can always tell when a certain class are out on that business, for they carry the anxious, searching look in every feature. They will begin to quiz, and tell what they have heard about Mr., or Mrs., or Miss such an one, and to know if I have not heard of it. All of that is to get something to add to the petticoat telegraph communications.

The northerner's brain appear to generate the same tyranical propensity that the southerners have in their power to carry out; that is all the difference between the North and the South. The northerners are growing more tyranical, while the southerners are ameliorating the condition of the slaves very much in some respects. There is one striking feature in slavery that is dying out, which is separating families when they are sold, yet it is not altogether done away with, but I think it will be eventually. I was told that a great many of them do not care anything about being separated, and some had much rather be than not, just like the white people in the free States. Others who have strong feelings of attachment, are the most subdued looking beings that I ever saw in my life, it was painful to see them. But a great many of the slaves have money, for they have what they can make by the variety of little privileges that their masters allow them. They have no necessary out-goes, but if they have nice clothes they pay for them out of their own money, and then they will take care of them. Many of them who are bright have nice Sunday clothes, as they call them, and plenty of good jewelry, and some money at interest. I very often saw the white lady of the house go to her slaves to borrow money to buy one of my books. I found they were quite as apt to have change as the lady of the house, and some of the first class slaves are very good capitalists, too. Each holiday they have one week to go where they please and do as they please by the way of frolicking and making their own purchases, out of their own means, as long as it lasts. Some of them are prudent, while others spend the last cent.

Last Christmas day I was in the South, on the Baltimore and Ohio Railroad, in a village of three or four thousand inhabitants. One merchant told me that he had sold seventeen hoop skirts to the slaves, and there was seven or eight stores in the place, and it is hard telling how many they all sold. I had hard work to get near enough to the merchants to speak with them that day, for the hoops were on every side; the negresses wholly monopolized the day. I felt very poor when I saw them make their purchases, and yet they were slaves. I met some Northern people there who thought slavery was as high a state of civilization as the most of the slaves are capable of attaining to now, and I know it is the case with a great many of them, and it always will be so unless they are developed to the extent of their capacities. I know that thousands of them would be very far in advance of what they now are if they had been allowed an equal chance with the white people, yet I did not see but a very few real Africans who were intellectual or refined. I saw a few of the pure Africans who appeared very manly, and who could read very well. That class are allowed the privilege of buying such books as they choose, if they were not anti-slavery publications. The white people would look for themselves, and buy if they chose, but I did not offer them any; I meant to be careful and not give offense. I knew there was a law to prohibit book peddling there, but they allowed me to pass for a long time after the Harper's Ferry insurrection occurred, because I was a lady, for the better class of Southerners are very respectful to ladies. They arrested a great many men peddlers, and fined them, and if the newspapers were reliable they treated some of them very hard, but whether it was without a cause or not, I am not able to say. But I can speak for myself, and I know that my ill treatment was without the least provocation in the world on my part, for I presume I was told one hundred times that I should have no trouble if I did not make trouble for them by selling anti-slavery books or papers to the negroes, nor talk with them on the subject of slavery. Yet a certain class in some of the Southern States made me a great deal of trouble, and all of it uncalled for. But I always took the privilege of telling the troublesome class that I had found out that all the mean people were not in the Northern States, for they were no better than we were. They said they thought they were, and I told them that was their ignorance.

I found all those who had traveled through the free States to be very friendly to me indeed, and very many who had not been here. I also found that the northern people who had traveled through the Southern States found a different state of things from what they expected, and those who went there from good motives were rather happily disappointed in favor of the slaveholder. Some that I met went there with strong anti-slavery principles, but when they came to see for themselves, their fiery enthusiasm evaporated, for they think there is a great field of labor to be performed before the slaves will be prepared for freedom.

I told a great many gentlemen and ladies that if I was able to do anything for the South, I should make it my first business to establish free schools to educate the white people, and prepare them to know what to do with the Africans, and then I think we should accomplish something. I think that the Northern people are exhausting their energies in a course that they do not fully understand, and I am afraid that they have taken some rash steps which will prove to be a great detriment to both North and South.

It is very true that the soil and climate of the South is prolific of a class of agricultural staples that ours is not, but we are by far the strongest people, and they know that very well, and they also know that it is our free schools, and free labor, and industrious habits that make us strong, both mentally and physically. Yet the white population of neither North or South can ever endure the laborious toil of the cotton and sugar plantations. Three quarters of the white population would die with sun stroke where and when the genuine African would select the very time and place to lie down on the ground and go to sleep. If there is a shade tree near them, or if they are in the shady side of the house, and wish to lay down, it is invariably the case that they will select the sunny side of the house, or the open lot in preference to the shade anywhere. I have seen that in hundreds of cases. But the mulatto, who inherits the white constitution, has not the power of endurance that the pure African has, and they generally make house servants of them, for they will not sell as high as the genuine for any purpose, except for house servants. If they are honest and healthy they are worth a large sum, perhaps from ten to fifteen hundred dollars. There are a great many house slaves who carry all the keys in the house more than any of the family do, for they are too indolent to have the care of the keys to their trunks. The white people often speak of their own indolent habits, and laugh about themselves, and tell how quick the Yankees move, and how much they know. They nearly worship a Yankee who goes there to locate, for they say they know how to do everything, and do not feel above doing anything. But the Yankees have made them so much trouble that at this present time it is very dangerous for a person to go far South; even if their motives are good they are liable to be arrested and abused every way.

I wish the North and South would hit upon some plan or other to agree not to disagree, for African labor is certainly more useful there than it can be anywhere else in the world. The cotton fields require their labor the year round, and they work on them all the time except a few cold and rainy days in the winter. I saw them gathering cotton in January. It rains there some winters half of the time; it generally commences in the month of December and continues until the middle or last of February. The Southern States will always be subjected to long, sweeping rains, from the fact that evaporation is continually going on from the sea, and in the warm southern climate the vapors condense in the form of rain instead of snow. They are liable to a variety of misfortunes from the effect of long, drenching rains during the winter months, and less rain there will do more damage than the same would here, because there is no grass to protect the surface of the ground, or no roots to the dry miserable looking grass, and the soil gulleys and often washes the railroads and bridges away, and tears other roads up by the roots at such a rate that travelers are often detained a long time, and sometimes they are a number of times during the winter.

I found it rather an expensive job in my business there last winter, for in a private dwelling I paid three dollars for two days' board. The old man of the house prayed over everything we had to eat, and one of his darling children stole a number of articles from me one day while I was eating my dinner. He was the agent in the depot, and there happened to be a trunk set off of the cars that was not called for in two or three days, and that praying man would not set that trunk from the platform into the depot, because the man was not there to pay him for it. The old woman told me that it was out two or three days, and then it was found a short distance from the depot broken open and all the contents taken out, and thrown into an old cellar. It was the work of the niggers, as the Southerners all call them, but I think that it was white niggers, who belonged to the same family that stole from me. That family were called an excellent family there, but here they would belong to the lowest class of white people. The most who keep public houses there belong to the very lowest classes by nature. They are what I call the vulgar swaggers, very low organized, and have very low, forcible heads, and just fitted to gather up money, no matter how or who from. I saw about seven or eight first class men in taverns, and I was treated very well by them, and I always am by first class people everywhere, but they were generally poor.

I often had some trouble to get my trunk taken out of the depot on to the platform, simply because I was from the North. They do not have baggage masters there in the depots, they have only one on the cars. I adopted the plan of telling the agent that I should not get a ticket until my trunk was taken out on to the platform, and in such cases I never failed to tell them that I supposed that treatment to a lady was their southern hospitality. It was generally the lowest class, who had any education, that were employed on railroads there. The best class are all on plantations. I saw a great many of the planters in the villages, and the most wealthy gentlemen were dressed very plain, and many of them bought books of me. That class of still, unassuming planters, are the cream of all the Southern States, and yet there are a few first class men and women in all the villages of any size, and in that class I found the hospitality and generosity. The other class that I have spoken of have not the least hospitality in the world, but some of them have generosity, and that covers a large piece of ground. But I always found that class to have selfishness that would cover more ground than their benevolence would. The people here generally think that all the Southern people are all as hospitable as the few that are truly so, for their noble deeds have given character to the whole. But we are mistaken, for I certainly never met so many people in one year in my life who manifested the over reaching, glaring selfishness, as I met in the Southern States. On one steamboat the clerk or captain took three dollars of me for only going twenty miles, and the established price was only two. I did not know the distance until after I had paid my fare or I should not have paid but two; that was a link of southern hospitality. I received ten favors North and West, and even in Canada, **to one in the Southern States.**

I sold books there nearly one year, and I only cleared about five dollars, and it was by far the hardest years' work that I have done since I have been engaged in book selling. In many places the slaves were more polite to me than the white people. The most of them are very docile, but much more so very far South than near the free States. On the large plantations they are not allowed to go from one plantation to another but a little, for fear they will plan for insurrections, but whenever there is a slave burned or hanged for crime, then all the slaves for a long distance are allowed to go and see what their destiny would be for the same offense.

They generally have preaching on the large plantations every Sabbath, if not all day a part of the day. If a slaveholder does not have preaching on his plantation the first class do not think highly of him, and the slaves say that massa is a powerful wicked man, and that is " zactly" so. Now and then a slave preaches a sermon to the rest, and he tell them " where de good massa go and where de good slave go, and dat is de place where de man don't nebber die, nor de fire is not squinched." In the midst of their ignorance there is a talent, and they are destined to live until the green grass grows over the sod of the slaveholder who now stands over them with the lash, to crush every aspiration out of their natures with the iron heel of oppression. There are very good mechanics among the slaves, and I have known and heard of a few of the mechanics being valued at two thousand dollars. Sometimes they will buy themselves and families, but they are obliged to pay a dear price for themselves, for one of them can earn fine wages there. But who knows what to do with them all at present, their help is not wanted here, for the supply is now greater than the demand, for low occupations, and in Canada they are overrun with fugitives from the South. They have not the capacity to take care of themselves, and they beg and steal, and I was told that their criminal institutions were crowded with fugitive slaves. What else can they do but beg and steal? I would not starve if I were they. They are making some trouble in Canada; it seems rather a bold push to go in and take possession of a public school.

I think that if every slave was set at liberty to-day, that in less than one week, or before next Saturday night, the majority of them would go back to their masters. They often attempt to run away, and stay around in the woods until they get hungry and cold, and then go back again. The nights are much colder there accordingly than they are here, for the dews are so much more heavy that there is a damp chill in the air which is very unpleasant to be out in over night.

I think that the class of evils that exist there are hard to be borne, and greater than they need to be, but I think to free them all now it would create a class of evils that would be ten per cent. worse for the slaves, and be a very great injury to the white people of both North and South.

I find that people who have not been there are apt to judge of the character of the slaves by the class of Africans that are brought up here, with northern principles, and by the class that are shrewd enough to run away. But let any man go there from the North with an unprejudiced mind, and see what they are collectively, and I know he would acknowledge that the Northern people had talked a great deal and a great while about a subject that they think they know all about, but come to the truth of the case they do not know anything about it. They are so crazy on the subject that they will not believe those who have been there. If you tell them the candid truth they are mad because it is not bad enough, and to reason with them is out of the question, for it is just like undertaking to break up an old fashion hornets' nest, for instead of listening to facts they will fly up on every side and stab one with their tongues. They will not keep cool long enough to receive an impression unless it fits the crazy bumps in their heads.

I was told several times that a slave always objected to being sold to a Northern man, for a Yankee always expected more of one slave that a Southerner did of two.

We allow all classes of wrongs to pass unnoticed in our criminal as well as our benevolent institutions, and we do not have meetings called to investigate and regulate our home institutions. The slaves in their cabins are very well provided for compared with the inmates of the poorhouses. I presume there are one hundred people murdered, both direct and indirect, in our institutions, to where there is one slave murdered in the Southern States. If their kindness does not reach far enough to protect the slave their selfishness will, and certainly at present, when slaves are worth the money they are, for the demand for slave labor is greater than the supply.

I saw some free Africans who looked very hard indeed, and I saw some who looked very well indeed, and it was the case with the slaves. In some families that I was in the slaves were certainly the happiest beings that I ever saw in my life, and I found the white people to be intelligent where the slaves looked happy.

Louisana is called the most cruel slave State, and I found the French, Spaniards and Creoles to be more cruel than the native Americans, though the Creole was less cruel than either the French or Spaniards. Between Baton Rouge and New Orleans I saw the three classes I have spoken of, and I thought the most of them were hard masters. One lady told me that a few slaves had thrown themselves into the river and drowned, rather than to submit to one of the whippings that they were liable to get, and that on the plantation near where she lived, there was one slave whipped so that he died in two days; she said that she saw him standing in the river to wash the blood off of himself, and that was the last time he went out.

I did not see but one whipped, and that was by a French man, and in the business part of the village, on Main st. I first heard the blows and looked around. The slave had on black pants and a red flannel shirt, and the master whipped him with a twisted leather whip, which is as hard as a flint, I saw that he struck him as hard as he possibly could, and appeared to be almost a maniac because he could not strike him harder. The old Frenchman looked more like a fiend sent back from the lower regions than he did like a man; but he was one of the lowest class of slaveholders. I did not dare to ask what the crime was, but he only gave him ten blows. The slave said something to him after he had done, and the old fellow shook his fist in his face, but I was too far off to hear anything that was said by either of them, or understand what they said.

An English gentleman told me that he saw a master strike an interesting mulatto girl a number of blows, because she went into the cabin before noon. He asked her what she went up before the rest of the slaves for, and she said she was sick. He said that he knew better, and he had a whip in his hand, and struck her a few hard blows, and she fainted and fell. The man who told me of it, said that he took hold of her as she was falling and laid her on the ground, and he said she did not appear to know anything for about two hours. He said he never saw a more frightened man than that man was, for if the girl had died he would have been tried for his life, for they are sometimes tried for murdering slaves if it can be proved, but they are generally careful about that.

While I was South I read of a case of a master shooting an overseer, even because he whipped one of his slaves, and there are many masters who resent a slave being whipped almost as much as they would a son. I heard of a mistress in New Orleans being under fourteen thousand dollar bonds for killing a slave. The gentleman who told me of the girl that he saw struck, said that he saw a man after he had been whipped, and he said that he never saw such a sight in his life, that he was literally cut to pieces, and that his flesh did not look as if it was on a live person.

But the best class of slaveholders all acknowledge that there are wrongs existing in slavery, but the good class cannot control the bad ones there, no more than the the good ones here can regulate the wrongs that exist between those who hire their help and the hired, and what is more true than that reasoning.

When a slave becomes helpless his master is compelled by law to take care of him. He cannot turn him into the street, nor they cannot send them to the poor-house. The virtues connected with slavery are seldom ever told here, and I believe in showing up the virtues as well as the vices, and then the picture will present some light shades. I do not wish to be like a jug handle, all on one side.

The Southerners take a very broad view of matters and things, and they are capable of looking at a great many things in their one true light, because they do business on a more extensive scale than we do. They know us and themselves, too, and we do not know either. We talk of the half cent, and some of them never saw a penny in their lives. It is true that they will take the advantage of a person, but it is more than the penny that they are after.

All whom I heard speak of Mr. Pryne and Brownlow's arrangements, thought that Mr. Pryne was a right smart man, and admitted that he was too smart for Mr. Brown-

## CHAPTER IX.

The first class of Southern people and the first class of English people are very similar in character, and I think very much of both classes, for if they think one worthy of their friendship, they are neither bought nor sold, nor influenced by the low and the vulgar.

I have had one such a friend in this place, and only one, but she is now at rest, and this place must know I lost a friend, for there was no fashionable tears shed over the ever true friend of the poor. In that nature there was a "balm for every wound," and who knew it better than myself? I allow myself to think that I can appreciate every word and deed, which was the greatest medicine to my nature that I have any knowledge of. There are two kinds of mental aristocracy, the active and the passive; and my friends always belong to the active class, they think of others as well as themselves.

There is one family in this place in which I boarded for a short time, and when they thought they were receiving favors from me I was very good, but when I locked up my things so they could not steal what little I had, I was an awful being. The man was a printer, but was too lazy to work, and allows his wife to go out washing by the day, and his two boys to go out begging, while he sits around and does nothing. Although his boys earn their own living now, their mother pays their father's board out of what they earn, and at the same time poor widows have been helping her support her family during the winter. This circumstance I am not knowing to myself, but I know they are not too good to do most anything, for I have heard her teach her children to tell the most base falsehoods that she could invent. Yet she goes simpering around like the most innocent young dove that one ever saw. She ordered me out of her house once, before I wrote my other book, because I was so ugly she could not get along with me. But as soon as I began to sell books she was in hopes that she could help herself, and she saw me in the street one day and trotted up to me, and with that fine voice and her amiable countenance, wanted to know why in the world I did not come there. I told her I could if she wished me to, and I went there, and she found that I remembered my friends, and that I also remembered my foes. The man wanted me to hire him to write a book for me. As soon as they found out that they could not take what I had they showed up their true natures, for the next thing I heard from was their only young daughter saying that I was a naughty old thing, and she wished some one would take me and give me a good whipping. She lisps a trifle, and it has afforded me so much fun that I thought it was too good to keep, and I feel richly paid for the expense of printing it. I think the woman is a member of the Unitarian Church, who were so very holy when they first organized the society in Syracuse, that they would hardly condescend to allow a Universalist minister to preach in even their temporary church, which looked more like a slaughter house than anything else. I know they could tell the truth in a shanty if they chose to tell it anywhere.

The class of Universalists that I have been acquainted with in Syracuse, are only the very dregs of society, and the very lowest class of them are first and foremost in the ranks; but I have seen their low vulgarity at home, as well as in other places where they make pretensions. But I like to hear their sermons, and am willing to be benefitted by them, but I think the place to begin to be good is at home, in their every day clothes.

Now I will go South again, into Tennessee, where there is a class of people that I call border ruffians. The class is not confined to men, but women pitch battle with who they please. A Mrs. Martha Haynes threw a board at myself, that was only eighteen inches in length, five in width, and one and a quarter thick, but it had lain in the door-yard mud until it was perfectly saturated with water, and was nearly as heavy as though it had been perfectly petrified. It hit my arm just above the elbow joint, and it did not break the skin, but it grew large very fast until it was a very fine size, and had a very dark complexion. As soon as I went into the public house the lady sent for the doctor. They all told me that she had to pay a fine of twenty dollars a few weeks previous, for whipping a small boy. They told me that she had been in the habit of beating other women that she could handle, and yet she associated with the first in the place.

I found a young gentleman not far from Nashville, Tenn. who was a native of Massachusetts, and he told me that he could not live there, for the young ladies did not know as much of even common courtesy as the girls who worked in the Lowel factories. He took a book of me and gave me fifty cents, and he told me that he hoped I should never be obliged to go there again to sell books for a living, and that he was going home in the fall. He was getting a very fine salary, but he had been accustomed to refined society, and their ignorance and snuff dipping was so very repulsive to his nature that money was no inducement for him to stop there.

But I cannot imagine what the young man would have thought if he had gone as far South as where they keep their packs of hounds, as they call them, to hunt up the slaves who run away. They are trained to the business, and when they catch a slave they hold him until they are overtaken. One man told me that the master always allowed the dogs to bite the slave well, as he said, before they let go of him. I did not see but one pack of hounds, and I think I counted nine in the drove; they were all by the road lying down, I presume waiting for a job.

I saw one slave who had ran away. She had one small child with her; but she did not go far. She had been whipped a trifle, and she was ignorant enough to think she could get away. I was at the house when they went after her, and when they got her home her child had learned to whisper, or she had learned it to whisper. They stayed in the woods the most of the time, and they could not get her to speak a loud word. They kept the mother tied during the Sabbath, and during the day on Monday, and at night they had a whipping in contemplation for her. The whole family talked of that with as much pleasure as though they were going to some festival, or some other entertainment. I found it was a very great pleasure for them all to witness the sight, for one would tell what they would do, and so they passed their brute like remarks on the case. One girl, about twelve years of age, told me that the whip was about half as large as her wrist, but she did not tell me what it was made of. I did not ask many questions, for I was in South Carolina, and there I found a hard or barbarous people.

But I did not have any serious troubles until I got into Georgia. I cannot tell the number who told me that the farther I went South the better I would like the people, but that was not generally the case. I found some villages that were settled by emigrants from some parts of the other Southern States, and farther north, who were first class people. I enquired the cause, and found that the most of them were either descendants of Virginia, or some of the eastern States. I could select a Virginian very far South, as they were very kind and intellectual, for they are descendants of the English, and wherever they go there is progression. When I got into Georgia I thought I should find intelligent ladies, for I knew that the first female college that was ever built in the world was built in Macon, Georgia.

But as I went very far South, in some places it was a perfect annoyance to me to make them understand anything about books. The first place I stopped at in Georgia was Ringgold, in the northern part of the State, about twenty miles from Chattanooga, which was a village of about eight hundred inhabitants. I was treated very well at the hotel, but when I went out to sell my books I found just three gentlemen in the place, and I sold but five books. I saw the low class gathering into crowds, and I knew by their looks that they would make me trouble if they could, and I did not know whether there was good ones enough to protect me or not; but I was not afraid of them. When I went to the depot, the Marshal of the city was one of the crowd that followed me into the depot. He walked up to me and said, "Madame, there is an ordinance in this place against selling books, and your fine is five dollars, and I am authorized to collect it." That was an absolute falsehood, for he was not authorized; but I told him that he would not get five dollars from me at any rate. He then told me that he would take my baggage, and I told him where it was, and that he would find two or three old calico dresses in my trunk, and a few books, and if the old dresses would do him any good he could take them. He then said that he should sell my books, but they would have to go mighty cheap. I told him very well, if he wanted money, or was suffering for means to live on, to pursue his own course, for I could get any quantity of books; but he insisted on the five dollars. The ticket agent and landlord interfered in my favor, and they did not get five dollars nor my trunk either. The agent was very much of a gentleman, but the marshal was one of the most dissipated, low-bred beings on earth. He thought if he could frighten me out of five dollars he could drink whisky for some time, and treat his low comrades once or twice, and he would have made me trouble, had not the agent interfered.

That same low influence followed me the whole length of the road, for they were a very low class, until I got to Atlanta. Atlanta is now large enough to afford a rather better class. I sold books there very well indeed. The marshal's name at Ringgold was Whitsitt. I was told that they had been in the habit of throwing stones into the passenger cars on that road. I did not have any more trouble on the road, neither did they order me to leave the place, or make the least insinuation of the kind. Mr. Whitsitt was very impudent, and made some very low remarks, that were just as false as they could be, but the agent was very much disgusted with him, and treated me very handsomely.

The first motive in the low, vicious class in the Southern States is to attack one's character, or I found it so in my case, and the reason they do it is because they envy all the Yankees. When the Yankee goes in there they see their own ignorance, and if they can make trouble for them they will do it. When they commenced their impudence with me, I frankly told them all that if they made me trouble I would publish an anti-slavery work, and sell it to the abolitionists in the free States. I knew that that was the most provoking to them of anything I could say to them, and they would string up a man for that in some places there, and I think they would almost anywhere in the Southern States now. But the last few months that I was there I received so much abrupt treatment that I grew as thin as a living skeleton. Every one that I offered my books to I expected low impudence from, and I had heard so much of it that the dread of it became doubly wearing. But the kind ones kept me alive, and I was not ordered to leave any place until I reached Orangeburg, S. C.

The greatest insult that I met in traveling over five years, was about twenty or twenty-five miles from this place, in the town of Delphi, by old Tom Fairbanks, as they call him where he is best known. I found they all thought him to be a despisable, not man, but brute, and I know him to be so. I have heard that his wife told their children that I was a poor miserable person, but such remarks never reach my case. But I pity the person who is willing to plant falsehoods in the minds of their children at the expense of their character, for it is quite enough for children to know that their parents are vicious. Children who have the misfortune to be born of vicious parents had ought to have the privilege of growing up as good as their natures will allow them to. But I was very well protected there as soon as my case was known, and I have heard that Mr. Fairbanks came very near being treated rather severely, which would have been just right for the old fiend.

When I was on the Mobile and Ohio Railroad, I was in a small village, and in the largest dry goods store in the place. There were four or five clerks in the store, and they all belonged to the low, ignorant class. They looked at my books, and I comprehended them very soon, and told them that I had no time to spend with the low and the vulgar. I had to take the cars in the evening; and before they were due who should appear at the depot but two low, vulgar fellows, from that store. They were both intoxicated, or partly so, and one of them walked up to me to shake hands. I told him that he was drunk, and I wished him to leave, but he rather insisted on being impudent. I knew I must be very positive with them, and very quiet, for I saw at once that the young agent was afraid of them, and the older agent had got so drunk himself before dark that he was not able to be on duty. But before he left the depot there was a Quaker went there to take the cars at the same time that I wished to, and he gave me an introduction to the Quaker, and I felt very well protected until the two fellows went from the store, and then I saw that the Quaker was afraid of them. After we got seated in the cars, he told me that he lived in Kentucky, and he said that he understood the Southerners very well, and if he had said one word they would have presented either a dirk or a pistol. I knew the agent at the depot expected it, but after a while he coaxed them to leave the depot. But while they were there I stood between the agent and the Quaker, and one of them tried to make an effort to boast of Southern chivalry, but he was so drunk that he could not twist his tongue around chivalry; he made out to get as near it as "shrivalry," and it answered every purpose of the genuine. He had to coin language that he could use on special occasions, or that fitted his tongue that night, or the veins of chivalry that he was trying to describe. It was truly amusing to hear him talk, but disgusting to see and to know the cause of his degradation. But I lived through it all, and am very glad of it, for I wanted to publish them.

After I struck South Carolina I thought I was in danger of my life. I stopped in a very small village to sell books, where the landlord at the public house was agent at the depot, and I saw that he was a very rough, ugly fellow. There was an old woman kept a boarding house, and her boarders were young men, who were considered scholars in that part of the world, but here they would be thought no more of than the lowest class of Irish. I went there to ask the lady if I could stay all night, expecting to find a better house than the hotel, because I heard that she boarded scholars, and I expected to find the best class in the place at her house. But I soon found out that they were the lowest class of Southerners, and the old woman was as low as they were. I told her that I did not like to stay there, and she said she was afraid I would not be treated well. But the greatest trouble was, that they did not feel at home when I was present, and the old woman was in perfect agony until she had disposed of my case. I went to the poorest family in the place, and told them if they would allow me to stop with them over night I would pay them for it. They did, and we all had hog and hominy for supper, and when it was dark we went to the table, and they had no candle in the house, but took a piece of what they call fat pine, which is yellow pine, and lit that by the fire and put one end of it through a crack in the wall of the room, and we had a very good torch light to eat our hog and hominy by. And then they began to regulate beds, and I slept in a room with two women and six children, which made nine in number, including myself. We all had but two beds, and one of the women and two of the children occupied the same bed with myself. The offspring were very sociable during the night, and I thought it was heavenly music, but rather too much of it, besides a great many discords. But they did the best they could by me and for me, and I paid them for it, and they appeared to think themselves highly favored by entertaining the "Yankee lady that knew how to make a heap of books," and they said they knew I must be "powerful smart." But there was not one in that house who could read the title page of my pamphlet. I did not know but what they would finish me up there, but I am still alive.

When I was in Tennessee, about thirty miles from Nashville, one man shot another in a store, or close to the door, and I had just stepped out of the store only a few moments before. I heard the report of the pistol, and it was so near me that I started off my feet in a hurry, yet I did not know that any one was shot. I thought they were none too good to shoot me down in the street in some places, for they were having a convention at the time in Nashville, and when I got within the neighborhood of one of their conventions, it was frightful to see the feelings of the lower classes called out at the sight of a Northern book peddler. A book of any kind, presented to them by a Yankee, was enough to give all the low class the hydrophobia. I have seen some of them turn pale and tremble as though they had the fever and ague, and I always left that class as quiet as possible.

I went into Columbus, Ga., and commenced selling my books. I soon got on to Maine street, and there found a dentist by the name of Cushman, and he looked at my books, but I saw at once that he did not wish for one, and that was right. But I never allow the class that he belonged to to intrude upon my time, and after a proper time I asked him if he would like a copy, for I had no time to spend with the class that he belonged to. I then went down stairs into a store, and he followed me and walked into the store and told the merchant that I was a humbug. I looked at him, and asked him if he knew what he was talking about. He said yes, that I was a humbug. I looked him in the eye and told him that he was a villain, and steeped in the blackest dye at that, and the muscles of his face contracted as though he was going into spasms. He had a brute nature, and of course my brain was positive to his, and he found that I was not afraid of him. He said that he would go to the printing office and have me published as a humbug. I then told him that he had published himself, and it would not look any worse in newspapers than it did wherever he went himself. He went to the printing office, but they would not take any notice of him. I had been there with my books, but as I knew the general feeling towards the Yankees, I thought I would call and speak to the printer about it. He was very polite, and said that he should not attack a person's character without a proper cause. I told him that when he had a cause to publish me as a humbug that I should not object to it. I saw all the printers and heard from them, and I found that they all knew Dr. Cushman very well in Columbus. I heard that he sent a young slave all over town, or through all the business part of the city, and kept him just before me to advertise my case by telling them that I was a humbug, as though they were all fools except himself, or they would be their own judges of human nature.

When I got to Montgomery, in Alabama, I went into a store, and the merchant asked me if I sold many books in Columbus, and I told him that I sold nearly twenty dollars worth in two days. He then told me about Dr. Cushman sending the slave around just before me to tell the city that I was a humbug. I was told that he had a very bad name, and I told them that he deserved a bad name whether he had or not. One woman stole a five dollar gold piece from me while I was there, and it is the only money that I have lost in that way since I have been traveling. I rather thought the place was prolific of as great humbugs as myself. I did not mention the money I lost, for I thought perhaps it was done purposely to get me into trouble, so that they could get what I had with me, for I had been there long enough to understand them very well indeed.

I went into Opalika, Alabama, and perhaps there was seven or eight hundred people in the place, and nearly all of them belonged to the border ruffian class. They told me that the man who kept the hotel and eating-house to accommodate car passengers was a very fine man, and had a very fine family, but I did not stop there during the night. A lady asked me to take dinner with her, and I knew she wanted one of my books. When we were eating her husband came in and began about the abolitionists, and told me if I was a man they would hang me there. I told him that I had found out that all the mean folks were not in the Northern States. There was a woman there who helped him along, and he tried to make me believe that I had disgraced myself by going into a liquor store to sell books. I told him that I met with ten times the low impudence from the class that made great pretensions, to what I did from the class that appear to be just what they are. I told him that they treated me very well in the grocery, and all the abrupt treatment that I had met with in the place was from him and in his house. He kept a drug store, but he truly belonged to the dregs of society and the woman who helped along with his impudence was as bad as himself,—but it was not his wife. She led off with John Brown, and she and the doctor would strike the table with their fists as though they wished I was the table. I told them both that the base of their brain predominated, and that it would be a great pleasure to them to take life. I told the woman that she would make a good hangman, and the old man said that the Southern ladies would not do as I did no more than they would cut their heads off, and then brought his fist down on the table scare-crow fashion. I told him that the Southern ladies did not know enough to write a book and sell it; but I had seen them drink whisky; and finally the old fellow thought he had got his match. His name was McDonald.

I heard that people in the place would get drunk, and when the cars stopped there they would throw bricks and stones at the passengers, and they had been known to fire pistols and draw their knives, and the landlord would lock his doors to keep the fighters out. Some told me that it was dangerous stopping there in the afternoon, after they had nearly all got drunk, for the appearance of the cars rather excited them, and they had a heap of fighting to do when they thought a car load of passengers and the old iron horse would afford them an opportunity to gratify the organ of destructiveness, which is always very active when stimulated by the use of ardent spirits.

Gibbs, the great pirate, who had murdered and been accessory to the murder of five hundred men, acknowledged that he never could engage in crime, or stain his hands with human blood until he had stimulated with alcohol, and Mr. Gibbs had a much better head than many of the low classes in the Soutern States. They have a way of punishing slaves in some part of the sunny South, by which I presume that one slave suffers more than all the men did that Mr. Gibbs murdered. They stake them out, as they call it. They take two rails and lay them on the ground, and then they tie the hands to one and the feet to the the other, and the face down. They then take what they call a paddle, made of wood, and they use that on the **naked skin** until they blister the skin all **over, and then** they take a rawhide and apply that until the skin is all cut to pieces, and of course it leaves the muscles perfectly raw. Those who told me of it said that if the slave lived through it he was not good for much afterwards. But that was generally done on large plantations where they did not value one slave much. Some may not believe this, but I had it from the best authority, from Southern people as well as Northern people; and those who told me of it said that after they had cut their flesh all to pieces they would throw salt on the raw flesh.

It would have been hard work for me to have believed all that I have written if I had not been South myself. It is only the low class of slaveholders that allow such barbarism, and there are so many slaveholders that are low and ignorant that there must be, and are, a great many wrongs at the present time. The most intelligent class told me that the slaves were treated as men now to what they were thirty years ago, for then they said they did not think any more of a slave than they did of a cat, nor one-half as much as they did of a favorite dog. A lady told me that in her own room, and her father owned slaves, but they were very kind to their slaves. She did not wish me to speak of what she had told me while I was South, for they do not like to have a Northern person know these facts.

## CHAPTER X.

After I had been South a short time I learned to comprehend the true character of the Southern people. I found that they had a way of covering up, or trying to cover up, all the wrongs to the slaves, and those who treated their slaves the worst made the greatest effort to convince me that all was right, but my own eyes were worth more to me than their arguments, for the general appearance of a number of slaves told me how they were treated and what their masters were. When I went into a private dwelling I did not ask to know any more of the white family than I could read in the countenance of the slave that waited at the door, for if the mistress did not regard her word or the truth, how could the slaves know right from wrong. The first one that I saw would be just as sure to tell me a lie as she was to live, and a great many of the severe punishments which are inflicted upon them are in consequence of their masters' and mistress' example to them. I was told that in some of the Southern States the slaveholder would allow their slaves to steal, and tolerate it, and even share with them in all they could get. It is often the case that a man will have but a few slaves, and there are cases that a few slaves cannot support the white family and themselves, and the white family must have a fashionable living if the negroes have to steal it. After they have been thoroughly educated to lie and steal from others they are apt to grow bold and venturesome and try the game with their master, and then they are punished, and after a while they are sold down South, as they say, where they are staked out. It is giving them a hard name, to send them there to sell, and it is a great luxury to the overseer to get a new one that he can whip and abuse just as he pleases.

The farther I went into South Carolina the more brute

like I found the people to be, especially to a Northern person, and much more to one who was selling books, for they were so illiterate that they did not know the difference between an anti-slavery publication and a work written on the Lunatic Asylum, in Utica, N. Y. I have read of just such a class of people as I found in Georgia and South Carolina, and I have seen a great many just as bad, but not quite as many who were as vicious, without finding more who were better than I saw there. I certainly never saw such a motly looking set of inhabitants in my life, that claimed to be respectable, as I found in South Carolina, yet their natures were ten per cent. better than the low class of foreigners who come here, but they are undeveloped.

I saw an Englishman there who was a hatter by trade, and he told me that he had sold hats in a number of places, and he sold the largest hats to the natives of South Carolina, of any class of people that he ever sold to in his life, but he said they were not educated. The most of them have what Fowler call bullet heads, which are called very bad, because the base of the brain predominates, and that class would find pleasure in abusing any one that they could get in their power. There was not enough there who were civilized to protect a lady from the North traveling with books to sell, for it was about the time the Charleston Convention was in contemplation, and the whole of South Carolina was in a blaze of fire. I never saw anything to equal the condition of things there in my life.

A few weeks previous to my going there they had had a public meeting, and some of the consequent characters had made a few speeches, and when they got home and were at the dinner table, they repeated some of the remarks that were made at the meeting, and there was a gentleman from the North present, and he said that if he had been at the meeting he would have given them a good whipping. He was a lame man, and was repairing pianos for them, accompanied by his wife. They flew into a state of excitement equal to a pack of their hounds in search of a run-away slave when they had got on to his track, and they gathered around the man in a crowd, and took a vote to see whether they should hang him or not, and there was two majority in his favor. But they cut off some of his hair and put tar on his head, and then put some feathers into the tar. They then telegraphed to every point where he had to change cars, far and near, and then the low rabble would gather around the cars and heap their low insults upon him. They do not know enough to stop when they get through, if they did even know enough to do that, they would not be such a set of perfect barbarians as they are at present. There were so few in South Carolina who I saw felt disposed to be friendly to me, that they were actually afraid to have it known in the place where they lived, but they all kept still, and bought books of me. In one place I only sold one book in the business part of the place, and the man who bought it was a German Dutchman. He was in a dry goods store, and making money out of them like everything, for he was not afraid to work. But when I left the store they had gathered around from the depot, and were sitting on the steps of the store, and when I passed by them they clapped their hands and stamped their feet as though they were applauding some political speaker, and all uncalled for on my part. I knew by their looks what they were, and was careful to be rather quiet, but not appear to be afraid of them. I felt perfectly independent, and they all saw that and it only aggravated them, for all who could read had looked at my books and they could not find any just cause for any ill treatment, as they were in hopes to. They lost the job, and that was very provoking to them, for they knew that I had the best of the bargain. I very well knew that crime would punish itself, and left them very quietly, but that their influence would follow me. For neither the man whom they treated as they did nor myself had made them any trouble about their slaves. I considered them to blame in both cases, because I was told a number of times that if I was not seen talking with the slaves, I could go anywhere in any of the Southern States and be treated with civility. I took their own word for it, and did not wish to talk with the slaves unless I had occasion to speak to some of them in the hotels where I stopped, and then I often saw them watching me. But I did not care for that, for I was willing that they should all know what I had to say to the slaves, but in the house I was more afraid of the white people than I was of the slaves.

The Northern people do not see slavery in every ridiculous feature until they get very far South, and into a large city, where there are slaveholders who are about the same as out cattle drovers, for they buy and sell slaves and drive them around just as cattle drovers do stock. In all large cities they have them for sale, and perhaps in a strong brick building there will be fifty or more for sale at once They will have a back yard for them to run out in the day time, but there is a tight board fence around it. In the front part of the building will be an office, and on one corner of the office a sign with "Negro Mart," or "Dealer in Slaves," or "Slaves for Sale," on it. There were men, women and children of all shades, from the jet black to the pale mulatto, and buyers bargaining for them. There one will see the true realities of slavery, and it was frightful to me to see the countenances of the class of men that I saw in the offices of the slave marts, for they looked just like a class of very excitable patients that I saw in the Lunatic Asylum during the time I was there, for their faces were red and their eyes looked both wild and fiery, and their manners corresponded with their looks. They would simmer when I offered my book to them, and when I went into a negro mart I expected fire and fury. I soon found that it was best for me to fall back into a negative state and hear what they had to say, but I generally made short calls in such places. A few of them bought books of me, but it was not pleasant for me to come in contact with them.

A number of times while I was in the South I offered my books to both men and women that I presume could not read a word, and after I had started away from them they would send two or three negroes out apiece with some low vulgarity, and those who sent them would be expecting a dish of fun out of the reply they thought I would make the negroes. But they lost all that, for I never replied to one of them while I was there. When we appeal to a person's sympathies they will show their true character and not until then do we ever know each other. A person has got to be very poor and unfortunate before they can know what human nature is in its variety of phases; I know that fact to be true.

The Southerners have a great deal of ostentation, much more than people in general appear to think they have. They can make a great many flourishes, put on extras, and throw themselves around, such spasms are all pretensions. That class never bought books of me anywhere, neither does a true gentleman ever make such a splurge about nothing.

If Gerrit Smith, or Joshua R. Giddings, or Frederick Douglas should ever go into the Southern States they would soon see a splurge that they never saw before, for the threats that were made about the leading class of anti-slavery men in my presence was enough to kink the nerves into all kinds of shapes. Yet the first class of Southerners rather respected Mr. Smith's motives, but not his anti-slavery principles, for they think that he is a great philanthropist, and means to be an honest man. They think he is insane on the subject of slavery, because they say he talks the most about that which he knows the least. But it is not safe for any of that party to be seen in the South, for no person can realize the feeling that exists in the Southern States unless they have been there and seen it manifested. But occasionally I met one who appeared to feel very bad because the North and the South could not live more harmonious, for they said the North and the South had ought to be brothers, and it is very true they should be, but at present they do not recognize each other as such. But I think they had better hang out the flag of truce and come to terms, for they are becoming more alienated every year, and all of the trouble could be suppressed in Congress at once, if they only had the right class of men there. As long as the North and the South both send a low class of fighting characters to Congress, they must expect that fighting and all sorts of disturbances will be the result. But while I am telling them what to do I presume they will have it all done, for it is often the case that people try to crowd their advice into my skull unasked for, while perhaps the subject that they wish to advise me upon is all accomplished and out of my way.

I have been told that when I left the Asylum the doctors told those who went after me what I could do and what I could not do, but they were for once mistaken. They were like those who sent me there, who, in representing my case, made such an effort to make it the worst case in the world, that they really overdid the business and committed themselves, while I knew all their plans and had my own fun about what a set of fashionable fools could do, and how flat they would feel when they felt outwitted. It was fun to see how mad they looked when I left the Asylum, for the plan was to have me start for the land of departed spirits when I left that establishment, and all that time I was planning for my other book, and I have lived to see all my plans carried out.

The old dame who lives on Elizabeth street was so very anxious about my case and her fowls together, that she could hardly get time to cook her meals, and when she made bread it was a long confinement for her. She had a window on each side of her kitchen, and every person that passed, and every old hen that cackled she would fly to the window with much force, for fear something would escape her notice that would afford her a dish of gossip, that by the time she got her bread ready to bake the most of it would be about the floor. She would have a street laid out to each window, and pretty well turnpiked up, for I could see fragments of half mixed bread in every direction, and the streets run north, south, east and west. Every now and then her hens are troubled with an epidemic that she calls poison. She thinks the neighbors do it, but I think they get the deadly poison from the food she gives them, and I think that all who have been inside of her domicil will arrive at the same conclusion. As the Southerners say, she gives her children a lick now and then, and a blow is a lick in the South.

I went into one sugar-house during the time I was South, and the sugar-house looked very clean, and the best sugar appeared to be made very clean, and the nice syrup that we get there is made very clean, but the black molasses I should not like to warrant. The told me that if a plantation reached a village that the white people could not keep a cow, or a hog, or a fowl of any kind for a long distance, for the slaves would steal them. They would devour a cow in one night, and every person was obliged to keep a very ugly watch dog on their premises. It is against the law to sell to or help a slave to ammunition or fire arms, and a great many of them do not know the use of fire arms any more than children do.

While the Unitarians here are sympathizing so deeply with the poor African slaves, I would like to remind them of the time when they poured out their fire and fury at me about twenty years ago, when I lent one of the members of the church eleven or twelve dollars in money, at a time when he would have been obliged to have sold his household furniture if he could not get that sum, for it was for house rent, and at that time I thought there were honest folks in this world, and I let him have it because I thought him one of the few who were left. But I found myself mistaken, for on asking him for it politely I only got short answers. Then I went to the minister and also to his particular friends, and I told them that my health was poor, and that I did not wish to make a poor man any trouble, and that I was not able to lose it, for I was paying my board, and that was nearly all I had. But I found that every one I went to to see about it lent their sympathies with the dishonest man. Then I told them what I would do if it was not paid at the time that I set, which was a very reasonable length of time. But they did not move, and the first communion day with them I went, and while the minister was breaking the bread I took my time to tell the treatment that I had received from one of the brethren of the church, and the minister wished me to be seated, but I told him that I should tell my story before I took my seat. I did so, and the next Saturday night I got the money, and so much for claiming my right which I presume I never should have got without doing just as I did. But the whole crowd of Unitarians have been in a perfect blaze about my insanity ever since that time, and there is as much brimstone in their fire as any other church in the world, and it only wants kindling with a lucifer match to make a great blaze. About that time the rest of the churches chimed in, and I thought that as long as they commenced the fun I must feed them a trifle. During the winter that John Newland Muffitt held a course of protracted meetings in the Methodist Episcopal Church in this place, I listened to his arguments for a time, and I thought they were not productive of much good, especially for young minds that were not acquainted with the laws of mind. I found a great many who took nervous depression for conviction, and I knew that often produced insanity. I did not wish to create a disturbance in meeting, but I thought proper to change the current of thought, and I got two rooster feathers and put them on a nice velvet bonnet and went to church. The mirthful class laughed, and the old sulphur sourcrouts were in hot water, but I did not ask them to look at me. Yet the rooster feathers attracted more attention than the minister's arguments, and dried up a great many tears, and suppressed a great many groans. Even the minister laughed, and I thought there was more religion in a smile than in a frown, and I still retain the idea.

I recollect of stopping in Lagrange, Miss., it was near night, and the village was about half a mile from the depot, and there was no hack running at the time. I stopped at the Lee House, near the depot. It was a new house, and it looked very well outside and inside, but I saw they were very mean people. I had been to supper before I stopped there, and the old man was so mad about that, because he thought he should not get quite as much money that he did not know what to do. I told the lady that I would take a room, and she gave me a room with one bed and a lounge in it, and I was very tired, and after washing myself I went to bed, and in a few moments I was sound asleep.

When I got off of the cars there was a French woman and two children got off, but I had never seen her before she went into the sitting-room of the public house, and her dialect was quite broken. The landlady found out that she and no money, she was mad at her, and at myself too. When she wanted a room they made up their minds that they would put the paupers in the same room, and she said they sent a slave girl to my room, and she wrapped at my door a number of times, but I did not hear her. But the first thing I did hear was a pounding on my door enough to break it down, and a voice both loud and rough enough to start the walls of any house in the Southern States. Of course I was up, and asked the old Turk what he wanted, and he said that was his business. I then told him that I thought it was my business too. I did not know what time it was, but I supposed it was late in the night, and thought that it was a slave insurrection. but in a moment I heard voices, and I knew they were white women's. The old ruffian, for I do not know what else to call him, kept saying, "if you don't open the door I will break it down," and as soon as I got on a few clothes I opened the door and inquired into the affair. The old man said that there was no place for that poor woman to sleep only in the room with me, and that I was a charitable object myself, and I need not feel so big, for I was not paying him for two beds, and that he should put that French woman and her two children in the room with me. I told him that he need not raise the whole town to do that. "Well," said he, "if you have a mind to behave yourself you can stay here all night." I then told him that he had better go off and behave himself or I would not stay there all night. I found the stranger to be a very fine woman, and I could understand her very well. But after all the noise and racket that they made they did not put her in the bed, but they made a bed for her on the floor. They could have done that on any other floor just as well, but they thought that I was out of money and they would make me a little trouble. They told me a number of falsehoods, and when I got up in the morning I would not take my breakfast there. I paid the old swine for my lodging, and then I took a number of dollars of change out of my pocket in my hand, on purpose to let the old fellow see it. He began to look rather more amiable than he had before, for money has power to subdue the rabid nature of the class to which he belonged ; but he soon found out that he could not get one cent of it.

I can tell the world that when a person gets very far South they will find that their money is their best friend, the same as they do here, but it takes much more of it to buy friends there that it does here, for it costs more to purchase anything there. But it makes the most of the Southerners mad to have the Yankees go there and make money and carry it into the Northern States to spend. If they go there to sell anything they like to have them spend their money there, and if they locate there they are apt to be very kind to them if they do not disturb their slaves, but if they do they will give them a certain length of time to leave in. This has generally been the custom, but in travelling through the Southern States with the present state of feeling, a person is rather liable to insults, a gentleman in particular. But I did not feel very skittish until I got into the interior of South Carolina, and I kept thinking that I should find a good class of people after a while, as I had in other States. I only found now and then a good individual, for the people generally were the worst class of bipeds that I ever saw in my life, except it is the very lowest class of Irish and German Dutch that ever came to America, such as have no authority here. But when I saw the class that were in authority in South Carolina I wondered what the rest were.

## CHAPTER XI.

When I went to Orangeberg, where the vigilance committee made it their business to make me a small dish of trouble, I found what they were, and I presume my case was the first one that they had dealt with, and they wanted to show very large, seeing they had a woman case for the first one. When I got there I left my trunk at the depot and walked to the village, which was only about a quarter of a mile, and sold books on the way. When I got near the centre of the town I saw a low crowd gathering, and I kept quiet and very patiently waited the result. Very soon two or three of the said committee followed me out of a store door, and one of them said, "Madam, I have a word to say to you." I told him I was both ready and willing to hear him, and he continued, "you must not sell them books here." I then asked him the reason, and by that time another of the company appeared who was still meaner than the first, if possible. He repeated the same sentence, which made it a heap stronger, in their estimation. I told them that I could live without their money, for I carried enough there with me to get away with, and that I was as ready to leave as they were to have me. One of them was a stub-nosed fellow, and he looked as if he had run against something and drove his nose into his face a piece, for just the tip end was to be seen. He knew a heap, and looked right smart, and his eyes looked as though he had washed them in glue water, and could not more than half open them. He asked the other if they should take my trunk, and the first one that spoke said that he thought not, and they both said that they should expect me to leave the first opportunity. I told them that I should expect to if I left alive, for I did not care about staying there long, and they need not undertake any very great effort to get me to leave such a set as they were. In order to leave I had to go right back to Branchville, to the Charleston junction, where I had changed cars when I went to Orangeberg, and I was very glad to get away at that. When they told me to leave I told them that all the mean people were not in the Northern States, and if they made me trouble I should make an effort to make it pay me much better than selling books had, during the time that I had been South, for I certainly should publish all the ill treatment that I had received in the Southern States. I did not tell them that I should publish the condition of the slaves, for that would not be judicious at all, but I told them that I should furnish the anti-slavery party with a chapter that would be a rich bone for them to pick, and more so because I had never been an abolitionist, but I thought I should add one to the party when I got home. When I went to the depot at Orangeberg that pack of hounds were on hand when the cars were due, but they kept out of my sight until I took my seat in the cars, and then, like all other low bred, guilty villains, they would dodge around if they saw me look out of the window, but I only looked until I saw my trunk put on board. They appeared more like wolves than like civilized men, for they all wished that I was a man, and then they would have hung me on the spot. I saw an old man take the cars at the same time I did, and I knew he had a message to deliver somewhere, for when he got into the cars I saw him look around. At length his eyes rested on my admirable countenance, with a look of revenge that told me that my case was not got along with yet. When we got to Branchville I saw the same man leave the train in great haste, and enquire for the telegraph office, and when he got into the car he looked at me, and the language in his eyes told me that he had done what he could to have my case attended to about right, and if it was not it would be no fault of his, for he had bugged his eyes out far enough to make them all think that I was a dangerous critter among the niggers. I had a presentiment of the arrangement, and when the cars arrived at Charleston it was about ten 'o'clock in the evening. There was a great crowd around the depot, and I kept my seat in the cars until the noisy crowd dispersed, and then I saw a quiet porter from a public house, who was standing in the car I rode in, and he was a white man. I stepped off the train and told him that I was alone and a long distance from home, and asked him if he would please to take me to a respectable hotel. He said he would, and asked me if I had any baggage, and I told him I had and gave him the check to my trunk. The moment he took it from my hand a man stepped up in front of me, and looked as though he could chew a bar of iron, and said, "you must go with me." I told him it depended on where he was going. "Well," said he, "you must go with me to the guard-house." Of course I knew what had been done at Branchville, and I asked him what kind of a place the guard-house was. He said it was a place where I would be treated well, and I told him that all I asked of them was to treat me handsomely. When he saw the porter take the check to my trunk he took it out of his hand in a hurry, and turned around and handed it to an officer who was dressed in full uniform, and the way he snatched the check from the first one that spoke to me was anything but slow. I then told them that I hoped they would secure my trunk, and they said that I should find it safe, and then the first one took my satchel, and we both took the sidewalk, on foot. I asked him what the trouble was, and after a while he told me that they had received a telegraph despatch saying that I was selling incendiary documents. I told him I was not, but that in South Carolina they did not know the difference between an incendiary work and an old almanac, but if they wanted to make me trouble when I had not attempted to harm them in any respect, I would publish the whole affair when I got home, and make money out of it if I could. I had worked very hard in the Southern States nearly one year, and had not made over ten dollars, and I went South without any ill feeling or prejudice against them, and felt perfectly friendly to all the Southern people. But I regret to say that I have seen fit to change my mind, and for what I had seen, not for what I had heard.

Perhaps we walked a quarter of a mile and arrived at what they called the upper guard-house. The gate was very high, and made of very large iron bars, and the entrance was lit up with gas. The ruffian who was with me bawled out "halloo there," and the reply was, "we are full here, you must go down to the lower house." By that time a hackman drove up with my trunk fastened on back of the hack, and Mr. Gentleman said we could ride. Very soon we arrived at another pandemonium called the lower guard-house, and the fellow servant who was with me gave another screech, and we gained admission. There were two men sitting at the table, and the one who waited on me asked me my name, I handed him my card, and he, or one of the men who were sitting at the table, entered my name on the criminal list. The man who was with me told the other one to give me the best room in the house, and he went through a hall, or the prisoner's hall and unlocked a door. There was a dim gas light burning in the hall, and a window over the cell door, or rather an opening, which allowed me sufficient light to see what was in my room. There was a thing that looked like a churn, a pail full of water, an old ragged sofa, and a few of what the Yankees call Indian blankets. The cell was quite large and high in the wall, and not really filthy, but rather dirty. At the top of the cell was a small window, but closed and bolted, and until after midnight it was very warm, and the atmosphere was rather unpleasant, for the cell had not been properly ventilated during the day. The cells were all in the basement, and one side of me there was an Irish woman who was very filthy, and I think the partition between the two cells must have been thick plank, for the perfumery found its way through some small avenues into my room to some extent, which did not strike the olfactory organ very pleasantly. I presume they thought they were doing me a great kindness to give me the best room in the house, as the officer told the one who waited on me to my room, and of course I felt best to feel complimented with the idea of being considered aristocracy in a slave State, where they know the industrious habits of the Yankees. On the strength of the promise of being treated well, I felt a strong claim upon the chivalrous people of Charleston after being arrested unjustly, but I now allow myself to feel well posted on Southern hospitality, and Southern chivalry, and Southern generosity, and Southern kindness, which are all milk and water mistakes, except the generosity. With the exception of a few cases, and as a people, there is no accomodation about them, not the least unless you pay them very generously for every trivial favor. There is now and then a humane Southern person, but the true character of the Southerner is, if one goes there with any money to get it some way or other. They charge such exorbitant prices for everything that it is almost as bad as highway robbery.

Now I will return to the guard-house again. After midnight I went to sleep on the splendid sofa, but during the fore part of the night I was disturbed by policemen tramping through the hall with some low and vile person, partially intoxicated, and screeching and screaming at the top of their voices, and that, mingled with the music which the delicate keys made in rattling against the iron doors of the cells, made a very harmonious class of sounds, which struck the ear very pleasantly, and yet the music was rather too heavy for the tasty establishment, when closely confined. When the officer unlocked the door for the pink who was next to me, I rapped on the wall and he unlocked my door, and I asked him how long they thought of keeping me in that splendid room, and he looked rather surprised but did not speak. Very soon I saw an Irishman open my window on the outside, and fasten it open, and I asked him how long they kept folks in these pleasant rooms, and he said until the Mayor's court opened, which was nine o'clock.

When any one came through the hall I would rap, and a number of them unlocked the door, and I told them I wanted some breakfast, for I did not get any supper, and they all said they would see about it. I told them that I wished they would, and very soon too. Each one looked surprised, and after a while the one who first spoke to me at the depot appeared, and he told me that I need not go into the Mayor's office, and I laughed at him. He waited on me up stairs, into what I should call the reception room. It was a large room, and very clean, but coarsely

furnished for a business room in a public institution. A
young slave brought me some breakfast on a server, which
was very nice and clean. I asked the slave to get me
some water to wash with, and he did. I asked the officer
if they had put poison into my breakfast, and he was rather
provoked, and asked me if I ever knew of their poisoning
people. I told him that I had not, but that I could not expect anything better of them. He watched me to see if I
had anything to say to the slave, and after breakfast he
went down and informed the Mayor that the Yankee prisoner was to be seen. The Mayor walked into the room
with a cane in his hand, and took his hat off, and laid both
hat and cane down on the centre table and took a seat.
He asked me if I was selling books, and I told him I was.
He then asked me if I was from Syracuse, and I told him
I was, and that it was the meanest place in the world, too
He said he had been there. I then asked him if he wanted
the key to my trunk, which was in his office, and he said
he did. They both went down into the office, and very
soon the officer came up after the key to my satchel. I
gave it to him, and in a few moments they both returned
with each one a key, and the Mayor gave me the key to
my trunk and told me that my case should not be published. I told him that it made no difference with me if
they published the truth, but they might rely on the fact
that I should publish the whole affair as soon as I arrived
at Syracuse. The Mayor then told me that I could go,
and I asked him where he expected me to go to out of the
guard-house, and said he, "sure enough." I told him that
I could not get into a respectable hotel after staying in jail
all night, and I should not go out into the city to lie to any
one about the case, and he told the officer to go along and
recommend me to a good hotel. He took me to the
Planters' Hotel, and I did not hear what he told the landlord, but I was treated very well indeed. When they sent
my trunk to the hotel it looked as if a whirlwind had been
through it. If they had been gentlemen they would have
got one or two ladies to have examined the contents of a
lady's trunk. And when they found out that it was a
great imposition on myself, they did not make even a

slight apology, and much less to pay the extra expense they had made me, which was not less than fifteen or twenty dollars. The Mayor simply told me that my books would not sell there, and I told him I did not wish to sell books where they could not read, for I had seen enough of South Carolina. I also told him that I left Orangeberg as soon as they told me to, and they were mad because I did as they requested me to, and I told him that I did not know what would accomodate their hospitality. The Mayor looked like a horse thief, but much more like a sheep thief. He was a tall man, dark complexion, and his temperament was bilious and sanguine, and a narrow head, and of course his feelings were narrow. I found they were all willing to lie, for the officer asked me if I had been sent away from any place before. I told him that I had not, but if I had I should have gone at the time. I told him I sometimes met with rather abrupt treatment, and referred to the treatment that I had received at Opalika and Ringgold, but told him that they did not even allude to my leaving either of the places.

I stayed at Charleston one day and night, and then left on the cars. Before I got to Washington I found by the buzzing around on the cars that I was advertised in the Richmond Daily Despatch. I made out to get the paper and brought it home with me, and the following is the paragraph:

In Charleston, S. C., on Thursday, a Miss P. B. Davis, of Syracuse, N. Y., was arrested for having in her possession incendiary documents, for which she had been sent off from Ringgold, Ga., and Opalika, Ala. She had been almost as far as Mississippi.

I was in Mississippi, and found a great many very fine people there for a Southern State, but the rest of the paragraph, except the arrest at Charleston, is just as base a set of falsehoods as any class of villains could invent, and if the Mayor of a large city will be guilty of the low, dirty, brute-like, villainous acts that I know the Mayor of the City of Charleston, S. C., to be guilty of, I wonder what we are to expect from the lowest classes in the city. I saw by his looks that he was a man of sinister motives, but I should think his self respect would have guarded him against doing an act of that kind. I told them that I had been in the Southern States a long time, and had sold a great many books there, and their advertisement would only be against themselves where I had sold my books.

It was amusing to see them look at me in the cars and on the steamboat, and in the omnibus. There were two or three Northern ladies along, and they all thought that I would be arrested again at Washington, and when we got there they were as pale as ashes. I was just as saucy to those who looked daggers at me as I could be, for I knew they were great cowards when near the free States, and I made faces at them, and looked them out of countenance, for they had treated me in such a manner that I did not respect them any more than I did a drove of swine. Such a class have no claim on my respect at all, for a class of people who have no self respect are not worthy of the respect of those who live for exalted purposes, for they cannot respect a motive above such as they live to carry out themselves.

There is one fact that I noticed while in the Southern States which I had forgotten until now. It is that when the Northern people go there to live, and even strong anti-slavery people, they very soon learn that the climate is so different from ours, and so little cold weather there that they are quite apt to fall into a languid state, and they cannot do the work there that they could here, and unless one lives in a large city they cannot hire white help, and they are obliged to resort to slave labor. I found a great many people who told me that when they went there they thought they would never have a slave about them but they found it necessary to fall in with Southern habits while there, for they could not hire a slave that was good for anything. Masters who have slaves to hire out will always hire out the class that he does not want at home, and those who hire have got to take the refuse of slavery, while the very best class is more than a person from the North knows how to get along with. The force of circumstances will naturally crowd a person into slavery in the

South, if he means to locate there, or make the South his permanent residence, for they cannot transact business to any advantage without the African help.

I saw many free Africans there who looked very miserable and poor, but I think that every slave in the Southern States who can procure a living for himself and his family had ought to be liberated at once. But reform to be effectual must be gradual, for an ignorant republic is much more dangerous than an ignorant monarchy. Education is a nation's wealth, and if white people cannot govern themselves it is not to be supposed that the Africans can.

The white people once attempted to enslave the Spaniards, but they freed themselves, for they possess a superior order of refined intelligence. They are full of native character and tact, and are apt to be rather cruel to their slaves, but I admire their general character. They take great pains with their own persons, both their form and hair, and when their children are infants they clip their eyelashes once or twice to make them grow thick and long. Their hair is very black, and shines like satin, and their deportment is dignified and commanding. Their general remarks are very select and refined, and they judge strangers by their deportment and conversation, and not by the finery that they wear, as the low and illiterate do.

When I see people exchanging looks and winking at each other when a stranger is present, I know they have no private character, and I avoid that class if possible. I have often seen the low and the vulgar effect what I call a villainous grin at the sight of a stranger, and that class are always full of vice, and are not to be trusted anywhere; but a lady or gentleman can look one in the face and you can see the truth in even the wink of the eye.

I found a class of interesting people in the far West, who are called the half breeds. I found many of them in and about St. Paul and Green Bay, and they, like the Spaniards, are a mixture of a number of nations. Those who were educated were very similar in character to the Creoles, and their true home is on Red River. Some of them are very beautiful, and although their skin is dark it has the same rich look as the Spaniards. The expression of the

countenance denotes so much native character that I was
never tired of looking at them. The half breeds were or-
iginally French and Indians, but now they are becoming
highly spiced with Anglo Saxon blood, which is calculated
to improve both classes. They retain enough of the Indi
an character to furnish them with a trifle of the wild ro
mance that seems to be constitutional with the Indian race,
which to me is the most to be admired of any trait in the
Indian character. The French refinement added to the
high tone of moral refinement that the Indians possess
makes up a very perfect character, and the most interesting children that I ever saw in my life I saw among the
half breeds. Their hair, and eyes, and teeth were so very
perfect, and also their forms. Those who were educated
never neglected their personal appearance. They are very
tasty in their dress and genteel in their manners, and as
the Southerners say, are a heap more graceful than the
pure Anglo Saxon, but not so mechanical as the Yankees,
but there is any amount of progression in them.

The people of South Carolina were the lowest class of
Americans that I ever saw in my life, for there were so
few good ones among them that I consider them perfect
barbarians, and no one can convince me that such a class
of people will be kind to their slaves. A great many of
them are inferior to the slaves, and when people have their
superiors in their power we need not expect to see much
humanity or justice measured out to them, but they will
double their diligence to crush that exalted pure nature
out of an individual who possesses it. Although I do not
profess or possess much merit myself, yet I have been
stabbed with long and sharp tongues so many years,
that I feel like a tin lantern, perfectly perforated. Their
small arms have been fired at my skull until it must be
porous, and charity has not covered my sins. It is only a
few dollars in money that has secured the respect of those
that I do not care for nor respect. But it is better to live
in peace with the world than it is to have disturbance
everywhere, if one can do it without sacrificing their better feelings. But if a person is greater than their misfortunes it shows that they did not deserve them, which is a

very happy consolation. All my misfortunes have had their origin in that which I was no more to blame for than a child is for being born with two eyes in its head instead of one. The idea of trying to force my opinions out of my brain is just as absurd as it would be to think of changing the color of a person's eyes or hair by quarreling with them about it. Belief and disbelief are voluntary conditions of mind produced by the force of evidence, and the former is not a virtue, and the latter is no crime. To use a Southern phrase, I hope that persecution for opinion's sake has done gone, for although the institution of Southern Slavery is a detriment to virtue, yet we have a great many features of mental slavery here that are equally as degrading to the white people as the African slavery is at the South.

Mind was made to be as free as air, and I hope the time will come when the yoke of bondage will be thrown off, and let the oppressed go free. But I believe it requires judgement to carry on a reform that will result in favor of both classes, the white people and the Africans. I wish them all well, although I suffered some in the guard-house in Charleston, S. C., yet it was a moment's suffering compared with the mental agony I endured the first night that I was in the Lunatic Asylum in Utica, N. Y. I lived a long lifetime that night that I shall never pass through again, and one sober reality was, that there was no force pump in my brain to crowd the water from my eyes. My feelings were crowded up to a point that cannot be expressed, for language is no expression of a state of mind like my own was on that night. But I was determined to be strong if I did suffer, for I thought I had a work to do, and I could endure mental suffering as well as others have.

I feel grateful for the patronage that I received in selling my other book, and I hope the people will remember me in the sale of this work. I do not recommend it to the public as a well written work, but a true book. As the old lady said she thought Mr. Finis must be a very good man, for his name was at the end of every good book, and this pamphlet is good as far as the truth is valuable, on the different subjects upon which it is written.

www.ingramcontent.com/pod-product-compliance
Lightning Source LLC
Chambersburg PA
CBHW021940160426
43195CB00011B/1170